BRITAIN'S
S...

S. I. Martin

Introduction by Trevor Phillips

4 BOOKS

First published in 1999 by Channel 4 Books,
an imprint of Macmillan Publishers Ltd,
25 Eccleston Place, London SW1W 9NF and Basingstoke.

www.macmillan.co.uk

Associated companies throughout the world.

ISBN 0 7522 1785 2

Text © S. I. Martin, 1999

Introduction © Trevor Phillips, 1999

10 9 8 7 6 5 4 3 2 1

A CIP catalogue record for this book is available from the British Library.

Typeset by SX Composing DTP, Rayleigh, Essex

Printed and bound in Great Britain by
Mackays of Chatham PLC, Chatham, Kent

This book accompanies the television series *Britain's Slave Trade* made by
Pepper Productions and Brook Lapping for Channel 4.
Executive producers: Trevor Phillips and Phillip Whitehead
Series Producer: Gill Barnes
Producer: Ninder Billing

To all descendants, everywhere.

CONTENTS

Acknowledgements

This book would have been impossible without the input and assistance of the following: Dr Hakim Adi, Kofi Awoonor, Dr Hilary Beckles, Dennis Barber, Robert Beckford, Professor Robin Blackburn, Ray and Edith Costello, David Dabydeen, Madge Dresser, Julia Elton, Professor Gretchen Gerzina, Dr Mark Horton, Dr Steve Jones, Akosua Perbi, Mike Phillips, Professor David Richardson and Lawrence Westgarth.

Picture Credits

A View of the Yacht Jason Privateer, Nicholas Pocock, *Captain Cook's Travels*, c.1760, courtesy Bridgeman Art Library

A Convoy of Captured Negroes Taken into Slavery, Verney Lovett Cameron, *Travels in Central Africa*, 1873, courtesy Mary Evans Picture Library

Negros' Canoes Carrying Slaves on Board, Jean Barbot, *A Description of the Coasts of North & South Guinea*, 1732, courtesy British Library Picture Library

Slaves in Hold of Ship, Johann Moritz Rugendas, *Voyage Pittoresque dans le Biesil*, 1835, courtesy British Library Picture Library

Slave Sale Bill – West Indies, unattributed, 1829, courtesy Hulton Getty Picture Collection

Slaves Planting & Tilling – Ten Views of the Island of Antigua, unattributed, c.1790, courtesy British Library Picture Library

The Execution of Breaking on the Rack, Captain John Stedman, *Narrative of a Five Years Expedition against the Revolted Slaves of the Surinam*, 1796, courtesy British Library Picture Library

Bristol Docks & Quay, unattributed, English School, c.1750, courtesy Bridgeman Art Library

Marriage à la Mode – The Toilette, William Hogarth, 1745, courtesy British Library Picture Library

Granville Sharp Defends the Rights of Negroes, engraved by Warren, after Clennell, 1765, courtesy Mary Evans Picture Library

Portrait of a Negro Man – Olaudah Equiano, attributed to Joshua Reynolds, c.1780, courtesy Bridgeman Art Library

A Rebel Negro Armed & On His Guard, Captain John Stedman, *Narrative of a Five Years Expedition against the Revolted Slaves of the Surinam*, 1796, courtesy British Library Picture Library

'Am I Not a Man & a Brother?' Unattributed, 1774, courtesy Hulton Getty Picture Collection

Kitchen Stuff, Rowlandson, 1810, courtesy British Museum Prints & Drawings Department

Lor! Cried Miss Swartz, William Makepeace Thackeray, *Vanity Fair*, 1848, courtesy British Library Picture Library

British Naval Vessels Attack a Slave-Trading Establishment in Mozambique, Unattributed, *Illustrated London News*, 1851, courtesy Mary Evans Picture Library

Monkeyana, Unattributed, *Punch* magazine, 1861, courtesy Hulton Getty Picture Collection

INTRODUCTION

There was a time when a child could be bought for just forty bars of iron, as long as she had a black skin. Happily that is no longer possible and we regard slavery as a thing of the past. But the point of this book, and the series that triggered it, is that the legacy of slavery still persists. We may no longer trade people but the shape of modern Britain would have been very different if England had not turned itself into the greatest slaving nation ever seen. Yet, even as we become a more and more multicultural society, this history becomes less evident than ever.

It could of course be said that in a society which has less overt racial conflict than at any time in the past fifty years we should let sleeping dogs lie. I have a friend who says that when he walks down the streets of a major British city today, if he is behind a group of teenagers, he can no longer be sure whether it is a multiracial group or not. They wear the same clothes, adopt the same walk and, in the age of the rapper, they adopt a kind of transatlantic, sub-Jamaican patois that makes it hard to be sure from where any individual comes. Because my friend is a curious type he usually walks past them quickly and checks. But among the generation which will determine the shape of 21st-century Britain, the need to know may seem more and more bizarre. For them, race is a less and less significant factor in understanding anything at all about another human being.

This is especially true in areas where large groups of black people have settled. Four out of five British people will live in cities during the 21st century. But unlike their forebears, most of them will know someone who has at least one parent born outside the UK – African, Caribbean, Indian, Chinese, Irish, eastern European. Many children will themselves be able to claim a mixed parentage. It will herald a remarkable change in the way that British people live and relate to people of different backgrounds, and it will constantly remind us that Britain is, if anything, a nation of immigrants, many of them African. However it won't be the first time we've been here.

At the end of the 18th century, it is reported, London could count a black population of some twenty thousand. Most of them would have been freed slaves, soldiers, sailors and servants of various kinds. The underground society they formed has been vividly described by S I Martin in his novel *Incomparable World* as a vigorous, ribald, buccaneering underworld. Yet with the odd exception, such as Peter Fryer's *Staying Power*, these people have been written out of all the accounts of Britain's story. If history is written by winners, then surely the slaves of the transatlantic trade must have been the biggest losers in modern times. The slaves were deprived of names, traditions, language and family – all the markers that make people more than tiny groups of individuals. Effectively those who survived the transatlantic voyage arrived in a new universe, where the calendar started from Year Zero.

It would be easy to put this down as yet another example of the racial bias and neglect which pervades British society. But this would be facile and simplistic. For a phenomenon as definite as the presence of so many black people simply to be deliberately suppressed would demand a conspiracy of monumental proportions. It is hard to imagine that anyone would go to the trouble. So why is it that for most people the presence of Black Britons so far back seems more like a mystery than a history?

The answer lies in the far-reaching legacy of slavery, both physical and emotional, in Britain. It is estimated that in the years between the middle of the 16th century and the abolition of the slave trade in 1807 upwards of ten million Africans were traded to ships slaving to the New World. Many more died even before being transported. From today's perspective it was a cruel, degrading business which shamed all those involved, including the African nations which successfully sold their conquests.

Yet at the time, in both Africa and England, the slave trade was just another branch of a thriving mercantile relationship that had been started by the sharp-witted businessmen of Bristol and London. It was developed and raised to a major global industry by the vigour of Liverpool's merchant families. By the end of the 19th century Britain had become the most accomplished, and largest, slaving nation on earth.

This was a huge process, probably the first great industrial-scale organisation undertaken by Europeans. Leave aside the issue of morality, and abandon modern notions such as the idea that a human being cannot be treated as a piece of property, and you have the elements of every modern trade. There are millions of seemingly identical units (slaves); huge factories (the word 'plant', meaning factories and machines, has the same root as plantation), a close attention to reducing costs, the need for large amounts of financing, and literally cut-throat competition.

It is, of course, hard for the 21st century mind to fathom the idea of trading people. But for most of those involved the slaves were no longer people in the way the traders, drivers, sailors and merchants were; capture had deprived them of the right to be regarded as possessing that special status we accord to other humans. Some argue that it was necessary for this to be so to justify such an horrendous transaction. But the slave trade could never have grown at the pace it did, and achieved its staggering volume, without the active co-operation of fellow Africans. This was, on the face of it, a trade from which every party, except the slave, gained. In practice, of course, it was not; though many coastal kingdoms did well out of slavery and trade with the Europeans, they failed to make anything more of that success. Instead the depopulation of Africa, and its relative lack of industrialisation, laid the continent's path to modern-day destitution.

By contrast the trade proved to be what Professor David Dabydeen describes as the hinge between medieval Britain and the modern state. Much of this was the result of unprecedented wealth creation. Looked at dispassionately, it is almost impossible to imagine how the glories of the Elizabethan and Georgian eras could have been achieved without the slave trade. Yet today Britain's contribution to slavery and the slave trade is primarily seen as the moral task of leading its abolition. The names we recall are those of Wilberforce, Clarkson and Granville Sharp. Even if we are better informed and have some familiarity with the slave revolutionaries like Cuffay, Sharpe or

Toussaint L'Ouverture, or the telling witness given by former slaves such as Olaudah Equiano, the story is still principally one of a great victory of good over evil.

There is nothing wrong in this, but, set by itself, the perception robs us of two vital aspects of British history. One is the deep integration of the slavery story into the mainstream of that history. The other is the continuing impact of the plantation economy on Britain and its way of life over the past four centuries. Put baldly, but for slavery none of us would probably be where we are now.

The British, as it happens, were slow to join the trade in slaves across the Atlantic; Spain and Portugal got there first and had developed a sophisticated system of barter with the kings of the West African coast by the time London entered the trade. However , lured by the promise of huge profits , the financiers of London established their presence rapidly in the 17th century. Successive monarchs, starting with Charles II, put their names to treaties that would put not only Britain's mercantile genius to the service of the trade but also its growing military might. The Royal Navy set sail to ensure that the transatlantic trade was defended from hostile powers and grew as a direct result of the need to protect ships on the triangular journey from England to Africa, Africa to the New World and then back to England. There was never any prospect that Britons would be slaves themselves but it was clear that, if they wanted to have slaves, they had to rule the waves.

However, the development of the slave trade had a much more profound effect on the future of Britain. We might well have had an industrial revolution under any circumstances but it would probably not have arrived as early or been as thorough-going without the slave trade. This is not just a matter of profits;

the very symbols of the Industrial Revolution were promoted by the slave trade and its consequences. For example, Matthew Boulton wrote to the steam engine's creator, James Watt, in relief that their fledgling invention had been bought by some wealthy West Indian planters. Without this support, would the two have kept trying to sell the machine?

The products of slavery, principally sugar, tea, tobacco, transformed the lives of Britons. For many, alongside the new opportunities which came with the burgeoning cities, the middle classes were able to enjoy personal luxuries that they had not made or grown themselves. Previously this had been the privilege of the aristocracy. Even the landscape of the country changed as wealthy planters brought home their profits to create vast country estates and new stately homes.

However, the deepest legacy of slavery is in the people themselves. A sober examination of the history of our slave societies demonstrates one thing beyond doubt: racial 'purity' is a fiction.

In the Caribbean slave territories frantic efforts were made to ensure that there was no mixing of races. Slaves were classified not just by trade or ownership; they were catalogued by race, as a means of ensuring that no descendant of an African would ever cross the line to become 'white'. The French even devised a system which meant that a new-born child which had just one black ancestor seven generations back, even if it had the blondest of hair, bluest of eyes and whitest of skin, could not officially be designated white. As we now know, many actually did 'pass'. In any event even those of us who do not look white know that not too far back in the line there will be someone who does. I myself can claim a white ancestor just four generations back.

Slavery brought blacks and whites together, not just in the New World but here in Britain too. It doesn't take too much imagination to work out what happened to those tens of thousands of blacks, mostly men. A few returned to the Caribbean or the Americas; most stayed and many had offspring. But the 19th century prejudice against a 'touch of the tar brush' made it imperative to hide the mark of the slave. The result was a black population which grew more and more unrecognisable as such until the memory of a slave ancestor faded completely.

Today, however, a new desire to understand ourselves is driving many people to look into their families' past. As many people who think of themselves as 'white' confront the fact that this description is, at best, inadequate, we have to call into question all our assumptions about who is what.

If you, whether black or white, are of the persuasion that wants people of different kinds and traditions to stay separate, in order to ensure the survival of our ethnic group, then this will be bad news. You are fighting a lost cause. According to the distinguished geneticist Steve Jones, the pure human genetic sample is an unlikely chimera anyway. Put more pertinently, some of the stories told in this book reveal clearly that, as Jones puts it, it is possible that 'hundreds of thousands' of people who regard themselves as having no relationship to Africa may be wrong. There is a slave past in many who would not have dreamed that they have anything other than a common-or-garden 'English' background.

There is a point in not letting this particular sleeping dog lie. As we begin a new era there can be few tasks more important than to know about ourselves. As we struggle to understand the nature of our nation, its identity and its place in the world we have to shine the light into every crevice of our past. Slavery may not be an attractive episode in our history but it belongs to all of us, and reveals that, whatever we think we are, we still have a shared past.

Trevor Phillips
London
3rd August 1999

PART ONE

THE
BACKGROUND

BRITAIN AND SLAVERY: AN OVERVIEW

The idea that human beings can be reduced to property is as old as recorded history. In all eras and cultures some form of enforced servitude was accepted. Slavery survived the rise and fall of empires and kingdoms. At the time of the Norman Conquest the Domesday Book records that there were 25,000 serfs in England – that is to say, 10% of the labour force. Before the 18th century there was no body of opinion, either from the Church or in secular philosophy, which stood in fundamental opposition to this practice.

However, the Atlantic slave trade was to transform both the idea and the reality of slavery by its scale and organisation. Slaves had tended to belong to a family, effectively similar in status to farm animals or property. Indeed, until the abolition of slavery in the 19th century English law treated slaves as property, capable of being bought, sold, exchanged and stolen.

Africans, too, had a tradition of slave trading, principally with Arab merchants, who would carry goods across the long desert trails to exchange for West African gold, textiles and slaves. For African nations like the Ashanti there was no moral stigma in trading people of another nation who also happened to be what the Europeans called 'African'. The tradition among West Africans had always been that transgressions of community or tribal laws could be punished by being sold for a limited period; people would return. It was only with the start of the transatlantic trade that a new phenomenon emerged: the slaves who disappeared. Eventually more than twelve million would take the trip from which there was no return.

In the early 1660s England was not yet a major power in the slave trade, though it was already a significant force in European affairs and the English captain John Hawkins had plundered slaves from Africa and Latin America a century previously. Portugal, however, had been actively engaged in the African slave traffic for more than two centuries; and Spain had built a lucrative sugar empire by importing slave labour to the New World.

The demand for slaves was driven by the needs of the growing sugar industry in the Caribbean. To begin with, England valued the Caribbean islands primarily for their strategic and military significance. The first Governor of an English colony, Sir Thomas Warner, was an ancestor of the famous English cricketer Sir Pelham Warner and the writer Marina Warner. He was sent to St Kitts in 1624 to secure it as a naval base from which the Royal Navy could command the approaches to the English colonies of the time and, of course, mount raiding parties against the heavily laden Spanish galleons carrying gold from their South American colonies back to Europe.

In time, however, the discovery that sugar, a luxury in Europe, would grow freely in the Caribbean transformed the significance of the islands. They became the destination of every adventurer, freebooter and risk-taker in Europe. Not all found themselves in the Caribbean by choice. According to Christopher Marsden-Smedley, descendant of one of the most famous plantation families in the Caribbean, the Pinneys, his ancestor Azariah Pinney was transported for participating in the Duke of Monmouth's rebellion. Azariah, having left his family's farm in Dorset to join up, found himself on the losing side. He came before the notorious Judge Jeffreys and was lucky only to be transported to the colonies. He spent several years working for landowners in Nevis, the neighbouring island to St Kitts, before his sister Hester bought his freedom. Before long he had accumulated enough money to buy land and start his own sugar business.

There were hundreds of families like the Pinneys in the Caribbean. Many failed but enough succeeded to boost the demand for slave labour. By the middle of the 17th century it was becoming clear that neither the remnants of the native Carib and Arawak populations nor the imported, indentured labourers from England had either the stamina or the knowledge to keep the plantations going. The answer, as the sugar planters of Brazil and Cuba had found, was to import slave labour from Africa.

But it was only in 1660, when Charles II helped found a new company, the Royal Adventurers into Africa, that England fully entered the trade. This company was granted a monopoly of the English slave trade for 1,000 years. Its backers included seven knights of the realm, four barons, five earls, a marquis, two dukes and four members of the royal family. The first ships took slaves from the African Gold Coast (Guinea) to Surinam and Barbados, a flourishing sugar island in the Caribbean. Two years after its foundation the Adventurers' annual return from slaves was valued at £1 million.

Despite its thousand-year licence the company was wound up in 1672. Following very minor changes in staff, shareholders and charter, it resurfaced under the title of the Royal African Company. Its credibility and safety was guaranteed by Royal Protection. The King's warrant was specific:

> We hereby for us, our heirs and successors grant unto the same Royal African Company of England . . . that it shall and may be lawful to . . . set to sea such as many ships, pinnaces and barks as shall be thought fitting . . . for the buying, selling, bartering and exchanging of, for or with any gold, silver, Negroes, Slaves, goods, wares and manufactures . . .
>
> Witness the King at Westminster the seven and twentieth day of September, 1672
>
> By The King

By 1689 the company had transported 90,000 slaves from the west coast of Africa to British possessions in North America and the Caribbean. The trade continued to grow. The profits were fabulous and many of England's famous names were counted as shareholders of 17th- and 18th-century slave-trading enterprises, including the entire royal family. Some other surprising names figure: the poets Alexander Pope and John Gay; the Duchess of Kendal, the King's mistress; and Sir Thomas Guy, the bookseller and philanthropist, who left enough money in his will to found a hospital in London for the 'poorest and the sickest', which has grown to become one of the most famous hospitals in the world.

This was a risky business but the profits could be immense. The stranglehold on the trade exercised by the merchants of London excited envy throughout the country. Several small coastal towns such as Whitehaven, Barnstaple, Exeter, Lancaster and Plymouth were itching to try their hands at this profitable business. But it was the merchants from Bristol (a port long active in kidnapping and transporting indentured Irish servants) who succeeded (by 1698) in breaking the Royal African Company's monopoly on slaving and joined in the trade.

Bristol discovered it had a number of specific advantages. Not only were its merchants practised at the business of fitting out ships; they already had experience of sailing down the coasts of France and Spain to Africa, where they had bought copper from the Africans. This had taught them above all that the Africans would not buy shoddy goods, so they went to some lengths to satisfy this new market with higher-quality metal manufactures. This was not a trade between civilised men and savages. The towns to which the Bristolians sailed were, in essence, pre-industrial settlements not that different from Bristol itself. The people with whom they traded were kings, chiefs and dignitaries. For them the trade was just that – a trade.

Competition was fierce and the Africans were canny traders. But the Bristolians were lucky. The supply of brass had always proved tricky for West Africans and had been part of the basis of their trade with Arabs, who brought brass objects across the desert. The Bristolians discovered they could mine the necessary minerals for making brass out of African copper from the hills around the city and within a few years dozens of small metalworks sprang up along the Avon to supply the African trade.

Merchant families like the Eltons, owners of Clevedon, a surviving stately home, made fortunes as the metalworkers made history. The support of the Goldney family was crucial to one, Abraham Darby, an innovative ironworker who dedicated himself to the production of higher-grade iron.

His experiments, first at Bristol and later up the river at Ironbridge, were the trigger for Britain's Industrial Revolution. In 1709 Darby perfected the art of smelting iron with coke, finally producing a metal that was both robust and machinable. It was the breakthrough that propelled Britain into the modern age. The Goldneys, who had made their first pile from a single, lucrative slave-trading voyage, poured money into his work. Darby himself later said he would never have succeeded without their backing.

This combination of trading, investment and modernisation made others, seeing the value of the African trade, study Bristol's methods in the hope of emulating them. Liverpool, a small seaport at the time, saw its chance. It had one great natural advantage: the deep water of the Mersey estuary, which could dock boats far larger than those dragged up on the shallow banks of the Severn. The economies of scale this afforded meant Liverpool could undercut the prices offered by the Bristolians. Within a couple of decades of the first voyages from Liverpool, which took place around 1700, the city was on its way to becoming the foremost slave-trading port in Europe and possibly the greatest transporter of slaves at any time in history.

So by the early 18th century London, Bristol and then

Liverpool, had developed into prosperous slave ports, sending manufactured goods to Africa in return for human cargo, which crossed the Atlantic on ships that then returned to England laden with sugar and money. The route – from England to West Africa to the Caribbean and back to England – was known as the 'triangular trade'. By the 1780s, when Britain shipped a third of a million slaves to the New World, the national economy depended on it.

The human cost was terrible. Though slavery in Africa had long been common, the deadly voyage – the Middle Passage – across the Atlantic was unfamiliar, brutal and sometimes unendurable. Taken from their homes, slaves were often packed into spaces too small to allow them to turn, with barely enough food, drink and air to keep them alive. It is estimated that 10%, on average, died on each crossing; on a bad voyage the figure might rise above 30%. Revolts and mutinies were common, though seldom successful since the slaves had nowhere to go, and offenders were ruthlessly punished. Nor did those slaves who survived the crossing feel fortunate for long. On the labour-intensive Caribbean sugar plantations so many died that new shiploads were constantly needed (the situation was different in North America, where slaves lived on to reproduce and grow in numbers). Black people also lost their ties to the cultures in which they had been born. Mixed together from different regions of Africa, without a common language or background, they came to be identified merely by the colour of their skin. It was convenient for owners of slaves to regard them as less than human.

The loss of humanity rebounded on Britain as well. The English had long regarded themselves as a people uniquely devoted to liberty, to the rights embodied in Magna Carta (1215). James Thomson, who wrote also the anti-slavery poem 'The Seasons', spoke for patriotic pride in the chorus of 'Rule, Britannia':

> *Rule, Britannia, rule the waves;*
> *Britons never will be slaves.*

Some Britons avoided shame by arguing that slavery had uplifted negroes, since it had introduced them to Christianity and civilization. The trade was broadly supported by the established church, and some denominations – the Quakers especially – engaged in the trade, believing they could bring some humanity to the treatment of slaves. However, many Britons were troubled. Humanitarian feelings grew in strength through the later 18th century. A famous, sentimental exchange of letters between the black writer Ignatius Sancho and Laurence Sterne, the author of *Tristram Shandy*, displays their common sympathy for the victims of the slave trade.

By the 1780s a wave of abolitionist fervour swept through Great Britain, led by the Quakers and, in Parliament, by William Wilberforce (1759-1833). The Society for the Abolition of the Slave Trade, founded in 1787, attracted many poets. A few years later the French Revolution, and the wars that followed, caused a conservative backlash in Britain. James Boswell, who had earlier argued the case for slavery against Samuel Johnson, wrote a poem advocating 'no abolition of slavery' in 1791. But Wilberforce won in the end and a bill abolishing the British slave trade became law in 1807. That did not, of course, put an end to illegal trade, let alone slavery itself. The conflict between the boasts of liberty and the actual enslavement of human beings passed from Britain to America, where its consequences would be written in blood. Yet the 18th century, which witnessed the high tide of the slave trade, also gave rise to the ideals of freedom, equality and human rights that would help to lead to the traffic's demise.

THE AFRICAN
BACKGROUND

The total population of the African continent in 1500 has been estimated at 47 million. Over the next 350 years between 10 and 15 million Africans arrived in chains in the New World. Four to six million more are believed to have died during their capture or the rigours of the Atlantic crossing – a total of between 14 and 21 million people. This excludes the 17 million Africans thought to have been abducted as a result of the trans-Saharan slave trade. History has seen few social disruptions on such a scale.

In the end, however, many specialists in African history consider the process by which slavery worked to be as destructive as the sheer numbers involved. The size and complexity of this human tragedy have engendered a number of sensitive questions which need to be examined fully before a complete picture of this traffic can emerge.

For centuries in Africa ethical conventions had governed the taking and use of slaves, who in most cases resembled the serfs of Europe more than the chattel of the Americas. These suddenly dissolved.

The Africanist Basil Davidson maintains:

> *The transatlantic slave trade vastly devalued human life compared to what existed virtually anywhere on the continent before. Things were not a peaceful Garden of Eden in Africa beforehand. But all of the evidence combines to show that the level of civilization in pre-colonial Africa was degraded and depressed by the onset of widespread violence related to the slave trade.*

It is this that leads us to one of the cruellest ironies of the entire slave trade and into an area that many Black people from the West Indies, North America and Europe are often unaware of or uncomfortable about confronting.

The institution of slavery, albeit of a very different kind, began long before the arrival of Europeans and continued well after slavery's abolition in the West. Moreover, the slavery of the Americas could never have approached the scale it attained without the collaboration of Africans. Most troubling, perhaps, is the way in which European perceptions of Africans and their behaviour lent an appearance of moral acceptability to the commerce.

The free-for-all among African societies to capture slaves from their neighbours and rivals for sale to Whites was deliberately stimulated by the Europeans, who anchored off-shore with their wares. And this same state of chaos comforted Whites in their view of Africans as ignoble savages.

The relatively small number of European merchants and

soldiers stationed on the west coast of Africa at any one time, and the quality of the firearms at their disposal, introduces an unavoidable question: How did several million Africans, mostly from the interior, end up for sale on the 'Slave Coast'? With the known exceptions of a handful of English and Portuguese adventurers in the 16th century, it is clear that few African slaves were directly captured by Europeans.

The spectre of racism lurks at the heart of every aspect of the Atlantic slave trade. Prejudice – whether liberal, reactionary or romantic – has fixed the template for most Western conceptions of Africa before the coming of the Europeans. We are commonly presented with images of African societies as being in a state of either 'Edenic grace' or total barbarism. Both these views disregard the facts.

The Africa that the first European explorers encountered included a significant number of cultures not so different, in many respects, from those the travellers had left. By the 15th century the interior of West Africa was home to a variety of sprawling kingdoms and prosperous urban cultures. The cities of Katsina and Kano contained populations of more than 100,000 people. Others, along the Niger delta, like Djenne, Timbuktu and Gao, housed between ten and thirty thousand. These city-states were trading nations and, inevitably, warring entities. The Malian empire, on which the Songhai civilisation was built, policed its vast frontiers with a cavalry 10,000-strong. Literacy was widespread in many regions. Luxury goods from as far afield as Venice, the Silk Road and the Maldive Islands were for sale in the forest-kingdom markets of Bono-Mansu and Bornu. The university at Timbuktu (as old as the University of Paris) was a centre of learning which attracted scholars from all parts of West Africa and the Maghreb. The standards of African metallurgy, in the production of copper, gold and steel, were comparable with, and in some instances in advance of, those of the Europeans. Within and beyond the west coast there were active markets in pepper, potash, salt, indigenous glass, woven cloth and, of course, slaves.

In brief, these societies were *not* primitive. An accurate record of the phenomenal increase in African slavery from the 16th century onwards must take account of the continuous rivalries among coastal kingdoms, local ethnic groups and cities in the interior. With the influx of outside capital, this pre-existing trade became fuelled by the growing demand for Europe's goods – fabrics and utensils, guns and alcohol. That slavery existed in Africa prior to the last quarter of the 15th century is a matter of fact. European involvement was to lead to what the historian Robin Blackburn has termed a 'degradation of slavery'.

This state of affairs, though long known in Africa, has become a subject of debate only in the last couple of decades. Kofi Awoonor, formerly the Ghanaian ambassador to the United Nations puts it like this:

> *Let us accept that we were part of it. Because the acceptance of the facts will form part of the beginning of a new consciousness on our own part. We did take part. We would be less than human if we hadn't taken part, because the greed factor was there, and a lot of kingdoms made a lot of money.*

Contemporary Ghanaian intellectuals are also reviewing their history. Dr Akosu Perbi, a lecturer at the University of Ghana, is part of a United Nations team charged with the world-wide dissemination of this information:

> In the fourth century AD Ghana became part of what we know as the trans-Saharan network of trade, which covered the whole of West Africa. There's also evidence that Ghana was receiving slaves along the trans-Saharan route into the country, as well as some evidence that from about the first century to the 15th Ghana was trading with its African neighbours, from Senegal right down to Nigeria.
>
> The first Europeans who came to Ghana were the Portuguese who arrived in 1471. When they got here, they found that there was a brisk trade in slaves between Ghana and her West African neighbours, and for a hundred years Portugal remained on the coast of Ghana and took part in this coastal trade, going to Senegal, bringing goods from Senegal and Nigeria to Ghana, and bringing slaves in exchange for gold. This was the situation before the transatlantic slave trade was introduced.
>
> I've been really amazed in my research to discover at least thirty-five slave markets in Ghana alone.
>
> In the trans-Saharan trade cola nuts, above all other products, would serve as the means for slaves or other goods coming from the north or the Mediterranean. In the latter part of the seventeenth century guns and gunpowder were introduced, and that affected Ghana because now people were asking for firearms in exchange for slaves. So the states which

were growing stronger and stronger would ask for guns and gunpowder, exchange them for slaves, then go back and fight again. It was a vicious circle, and this is where we find the precipitation of warfare. Those who were stronger would grow stronger, those who were weaker would grow weaker. And it's very, very interesting – in the eighteenth century, Ghana, which was known as the Gold Coast because of its wealth in gold, became practically a slave coast, because Ghana was even exchanging gold for slaves. It was a case of carrying coals to Newcastle. This was the effect of the Atlantic slave trade on Ghana.

A more personal insight into the human cost of these ethnic conflicts comes from one of the few authentic voices of slave witness from the period. Olaudah Equiano describes the capture of himself and his sister from their Ibo family compound by fellow Africans:

One day as I was watching at the top of a tree in our yard, I saw one of those people come into the yard of our next neighbour but one, to kidnap, there being many stout young people in it. Immediately, on this, I gave the alarm of the rogue, and he was surrounded by the stoutest of them, who entangled him with cords, so that he could not escape till some of the grown people came and secured him. But alas! Ere long it was my fate to be thus attacked, and to be carried off, when none of the grown people were nigh. One day, when all of our people were gone out to their works as usual, and only I and my dear sister were left to mind the house, two men and a woman got over our walls and in a moment seized us both; and, without giving us time to cry out, or make resistance, they stopped our mouths, tied our hands and ran off with us into the nearest wood; and continued to carry us as far as they could, till night came on, when we reached a small house, where the robbers halted for refreshment and spent the night. We were then unbound but were unable to take any food; and, being quite overpowered by fatigue and grief, our only relief was some sleep, which allayed our misfortunes for a short time.

The only reliable European account of the grisly business of the slave caravans comes from the explorer Mungo Park travelling in the 1790s. Of the indigenous slave markets he wrote:

There are indeed regular markets where the value of a slave in the eye of an African purchaser increases in proportion to his distance from his native kingdom.

Writing on behalf of the Africa Association, he reported that a typical column of slaves would spend eight hours a day on the road and cover approximately twenty miles. Slaves were joined in pairs at the leg and a chain would attach them, one to another, at the neck. Park accompanied one such caravan from the banks of the Niger to the River Gambia and was touched by the humanity of his fellow travellers who were 'doomed . . . to a life of captivity and slavery in a foreign land':

During a wearisome peregrination of more than five hundred British miles, exposed to the burning rays of a

tropical sun, these poor slaves, amidst their own in-
definitely greater sufferings, would commiserate mine;
and frequently of their own accord, bring water to
quench my thirst and, at night, collect branches and
leaves to prepare me a bed in the wilderness.

The slaves' ultimate African destination would be one of the European forts on the coast, such as Elmina, Bence Island or the greatly feared island of Gorée. Within their walls the young African captives would languish, for perhaps months, in overcrowded, foetid dungeons. Conflict between different ethnic groups and between Africans and their European masters was the norm. Revolts were commonplace, and their brutal and bloody suppression routine.

Gorée, blessed with a pleasant climate and an abundance of fish, fresh water and foodstuffs, lay within a tuck of the coast of Cape Verde. Its history was typical of the many European forts and castles which dotted the Atlantic seaboard. First claimed by the Portuguese, its ownership alternated among the Dutch, the English and the French. Gorée was also famed among European traders for its many fine houses. In a similar style Bence Island, in an estuary of the River Sierra Leone, had been occupied by the British since the 1670s, when it had come under the ownership of the Royal Africa Company. A golf course had been built among the slave-pens and fortifications where the wealthy – and predominantly Scottish – traders (attended by tartan-clad African caddies) could distract themselves between cargoes.

The fort of Elmina in Ghana was the focal point of the southern trade which encompassed the area from Senegal down to Nigeria. It was also the focal point for the trade across the

Sahara from the Ashanti territories to the north.

The coastal areas and tributaries between the forts and castles were also home to a great many solo traders. Many of them, like Thomas Corker of Falmouth and Richard Brew of Liverpool (whose existing Black-Liverpudlian family we will encounter in a later chapter), married into local African families, whose mixed-race descendants would continue slaving long after abolition was declared in Britain. One stretch of the River Sherbro was even known as 'Black Liverpool'.

For most of the slaves the moment of greatest terror was when they found themselves crowded together in the canoes that were to transport them to the ships lying at anchor on the open seas. One slave-ship captain, Thomas Phillips, left this account:

> *When our slaves were come to the seaside, our canoes were ready to carry them off to the longboat if the sea permitted, and she conveyed them aboard ship, where the men were all put in irons, two and two shackled together, to prevent their mutiny or swimming ashore. The negroes are so wilful and loath to leave their own country that they have often leapt out of canoes, boat and ship into the sea, and kept underwater till they were drowned, to avoid being taken up and saved . . . they having a more dreadful apprehension of Barbados than we have of hell . . .*

Dahomey was one of the largest African kingdoms to arise between the 17th and 18th centuries. Spanish travellers in the 1660s, noting the populous nature of its towns, remarked that 'the squares, streets and roads form a continuous ant-hill'.

Dahomey's pre-eminence along the Volta estuary is directly attributable to its trade in slaves to transatlantic markets. By the second half of the 18th century, with 9,000 slaves going to market annually, slavery had become the kingdom's greatest source of revenue. King Tegebesu's yearly income from slaves was estimated, in 1750, to be close to £250,000. When the Dahomeyan slaving enterprise experienced a dip in the latter years of the century, King Adandozan sent emissaries to Brazil and Lisbon in an effort to drum up trade.

Dr Perbi recognises the importance of this episode to the African community world-wide and West Africa in particular, in understanding its past:

> *In teaching the subject of the slave trade in Ghana I offer my students the privilege of knowing about the internal and the external. What I do is to start with the internal, because I've done a lot of research on it. When you start with the internal you also give them a general survey of slavery, so they have the background before the transatlantic comes into effect. That way they're able to put it in its proper perspective.*
>
> *The first fact that I always tell them is that slavery is a world-wide institution; it has existed from ancient times to modern times, in the most primitive and coastal societies, and in the most civilised. And then I tell them that it existed in ancient Greece, Rome and Europe in the Middle Ages and the modern period. Then I tell them about the indigenous system and move on to the transatlantic, so they are able to understand it.*
>
> *But, of course, when it comes to the trans-*

atlantic I will talk about the social effects, depopulation and the marring of family ties. They usually tend to get very angry at these negative effects. We are still not happy to call it trade but that's what it was. It was trading, right from the fifteenth to the nineteenth century. First the gold trade, then the seventeenth-century slave trade, then, through nineteenth-century abolition, back to gold, cocoa and rubber. Just trade. And some African people lived a wealthy kind of life from it.

But you have more negative effects than positive. And right now the legacy of the slave trade is still with us, because it affected the whole of Africa and Ghana. One of these legacies in Ghana and in Africa is the issue of economic under-development. We must remember that slavery was abolished in 1807, but in this part of the world the whole process took about a hundred years to come into effect. So we are talking really about 1907, 1908 when it all ended, and we are in 1999. So we are living ninety years after the fact, and it takes a long time to build up what we've destroyed. Remember that for about 400 years this had been going on. We've destroyed a lot of things, socially, economically, politically. So we are now building up and it's not surprising that we still suffer the effects. There are still some areas in the northern part of Ghana which are depopulated right now because of the transatlantic slave trade. And there are still some families who can remember the social relationships whereby this person did this to us, this family did this to us, and this ethnic group did that to

us. So we are putting up with this legacy right now.
And it's important to realise that. But the point is, as
historians, we have to tell the story as it was so that we
don't repeat the mistakes of the past.

The legacy of this era of African history still resonates
throughout the Diaspora. One of Ghana's foremost historians,
Professor Der, summarises the situation:

At the moment most Black people are still feeling the
psychological effects of the slave trade. Even in Ghana
the psychological effect is still there. There are people of
slave backgrounds, even today, who find it difficult to
participate in certain social events. For example, a
person of slave status cannot be a chief, he cannot sit
on a chief's stool. And now we have people who were
brought in as slaves from northern Ghana centuries
ago who have been integrated into noble society; some
of their grandmothers married Akan royals and so they
feel they have the right to sit on stools. But because of
this slave legacy, they cannot sit on these stools.

The other psychological effect is that people
from slave origins just tend to hide their background.
They don't want that to come out because community
people will discover that their grandparents at one
point were slaves.

So, anywhere slavery has been practised,
whether you're a slave owner, or whether you're a
slave descendant, you must feel guilt, and if you are a
descendant of a slave you will, of course, feel deeply.
Everywhere in the world the legacy lives with us. But I

think we should talk about it – to know the full story, not to distort it. Tell it as it is. And then it will become healing for all of us.

PART TWO

THE WORKING
OF THE SLAVE
TRADE

THE
PLANTATIONS

Olaudah Equiano has left a haunting description of the over-whelming sense of dislocation felt by the slaves at the point of embarkation:

> *When I was carried on board, I was immediately handled and tossed up to see if I were sound by some of the crew; and I was now persuaded that I had gotten into a world of bad spirits and that they were going to kill me. Their complexions too, differing so much from ours, their long hair and the language they spoke, which was different from any I had ever heard, united to confirm me in this belief. Indeed, such were the horrors of my views and fears at the moment that, if ten thousand worlds had been my own, I would have freely parted with them all to have exchanged my condition with that of the meanest slave in my own country.*

The average slave voyage from the West African coast to the Caribbean took six to eight weeks. The mortality rate across the Middle Passage varied from week to week. It was highest in the first part of the voyage, where disease, psychological trauma and illness were commonplace. There was also a tendency to throw the sicker Africans overboard when there was any sign of serious illness, so as to protect the rest of the 'cargo'.

These new terrors and the inhuman discipline which accompanied them were a foretaste of the misery which awaited the Africans in the New World. The accounts of slave-ship captains, of course, differ considerably from those of their captives. Speaking before the House of Commons, Captain Thomas Tobin likened the conditions on board his ship to those of 'a nursery in any private family'. Apparently the whole crew busied themselves 'making everything as comfortable as could possibly be for the slaves'.

By some estimates up to 30% of the Africans shipped across the Atlantic did not make it. Equiano's account of the horrors of the Middle Passage makes it a wonder the figure was not higher:

> *I was soon put down under the decks, and there I received such a salutation in my nostrils as I had never experienced in my life; so that, with the loathsome stench and crying together, I became so sick and low that I was not able to eat, nor had I the least desire to taste anything. I now wished for the last friend, Death, to relieve me; but soon, to my grief, two of the white men offered me eatables; and, on my refusing to eat, one of them held me fast by the hands and laid me across, I think, the windlass, and tied my feet, whilst*

the other flogged me severely. I had never experienced
anything of this kind before; and, although not being
used to the water, I naturally feared that element the
first time I saw it; yet, nevertheless, could I have got
over the nettings, I would have jumped over the side,
but I could not; and besides, the crew used to watch us
closely who were not chained down to the decks, lest
we should leap into the water; and I have seen some of
these poor African prisoners most severely cut for
attempting to do so, and hourly whipped for not
eating.

Food, when it did appear, consisted mostly of starch: biscuit, flour, yam and beans flavoured with palm oil and hot peppers. There were occasional concessions of salt beef and lime juice.

Not everyone could survive such routine torture and deprivation, and the weak were quickly broken, both physically and mentally. Inevitably a level of insanity grew among the slaves during the passage, and there is considerable evidence from the slave owners that many Africans arrived in the New World mentally deranged. Equiano now goes below-decks, into the belly of the beast, the slave-hold:

The stench of the hold . . . was so intolerably loath-
some that it was dangerous to remain there for any
time, and some of us had been permitted to stay on the
deck for the fresh air; but now that the whole ship's
cargo were confined together, it became absolutely
pestilential. The closeness of the place and the heat of
the climate, added to the number in the ship which was

so crowded that each had scarcely room to turn himself, almost suffocated us. This produced copious perspirations, so that the air soon became unfit for respiration, from a variety of loathsome smells, and brought on a sickness among the slaves, of which many died, thus falling victims to the improvident avarice, as I may call it, of their purchasers. This wretched situation was again aggravated by the galling of the chains, now become insupportable; and the filth of the necessary tubs, into which the children often fell and were rendered almost suffocated. The shrieks of the women, and the groans of the dying, rendered the whole a scene of horror almost inconceivable.

Languishing below-decks were people thrown together from very different environments. They came from societies with different languages and cultures, some of which had recently been at war with each other. Finding themselves in this strange new space, they had to create a new identity, a new sense of themselves, new ways of communicating. The intellectual challenge for them was to forge a survival strategy in very difficult circumstances.

The next great hurdle for the captives involved another stage of separation. From the moment the ships docked in the New World ports, slaves were organised into groups and taken to market. Here the auction block was the centre of all activity. Slave owners who lived in the countryside were usually given the opportunity to arrive in town in time for the sale. In some societies laws were passed that slaves should not be sold within twenty-four hours of arrival. Public auctions were the most common method of dispersal, but there were also direct consignments, by which some slave owners made arrangements with merchants to bring slaves directly to them, on the basis of a given number of slaves per year. Slaves deemed unfit for sale were classed as 'refuse' and were left to perish where they lay in the docks.

As with all commercial transactions, the buyers soon developed preferences. It was believed that the Mandingos (Muslims from the Senegal area) tended to be very effective and loyal slaves if well treated and if their pride and dignity were respected. But, if they were abused, physically or mentally, they were likely to be violent in their responses. The Wolofs, also from Senegal, were supposed to be diligent and industrious workers because they came from highly developed agricultural economies and understood the science of tropical agriculture; they were also open to incentives. This kind of stereotyping permeated the colonies but was far too general to be accurate. When it came to slave resistance all ethnic groups were involved.

Beyond the struggle for physical survival in captivity, the greatest crisis to afflict African societies in the New World was the break-up of the family unit. Having already been split, either in Africa or during the crossing, where men and women were separated, and then split again when they were sold as slaves, African families had little or no chance to re-establish themselves on the estates and plantations. There they were viewed as chattels, not as persons in law, and no thought was given to the reconstruction of slave families.

Family structure on the plantations remained chaotic. Not only had the slaves been removed from their African traditions but there were active prohibitions against them being joined in Christian marriage. Despite these conditions some 17th-century visitors to the Caribbean, like Richard Blagan in Barbados and Hans Sloane in Jamaica, testified that in the early stage of plantation construction the sex ratios were surprisingly balanced and that slaves lived in families. Adultery was punishable under communal law. There was, according to Blagan, no wantonness or looseness.

Further rifts would be driven through the slave populations by the grades of servitude, each with its corresponding privileges and scales of punishment. There was a clear difference between factory slaves, field workers and domestics; there were differences in status based upon place of origin; and there were tensions between newly arrived Africans, slaves who had been born and raised in the colonies, and the growing community of mixed-race people.

It is hardly surprising there was no immediate feeling of Black ethnicity among them. Such ideas were not to flourish until the 1780s by which time the slaves had developed a common language (patois), customs and aspirations. By 1750, the ratio of Blacks to Whites in Jamaica was roughly 10:1 despite the strictures of the Deficiency Act, which stated that a certain number of Whites should be imported into the island as indentured labourers to keep a balance between the White and Black populations. Internal divisions among the Blacks clearly worked to the advantage of the planters (who were ever mindful of rebellions) and became critical to the maintenance of discipline on the estates.

Where management techniques failed, cruder controls would be brought to bear, including floggings, the stocks, chains and neck clamps. Laws were also in place under which Blacks who raised their hands to strike Whites would suffer amputation of the offending limb.

*

The doubly subordinate position of women in a chattel slavery system also served as a useful weapon in the planter's armoury. Sexual abuse and rape were endemic. The diaries of Thomas Thistlewood (a former overseer at Vineyard Pen, who rose to become master at Breadnut Island Pen and Egypt Plantation) show how casual this exploitation was. Thistlewood, who celebrated every birthday by deflowering an African virgin, used his slave housekeeper, Febal, as his official mistress. She was also empowered to act on his behalf in his absence and had permission to ride a horse, an activity normally strongly discouraged among slaves.

On every property he owned or ran Thistlewood sexually abused enslaved women. He would describe in graphic detail where he abused them – whether in the great house, the smaller house or in the cane fields. Such impure connections often led to the trauma of slave women bearing the children of their oppressors. Normally the child of an enslaved woman was automatically a slave but there were several cases of slave owners freeing their mixed-race children.

This bestowal of freedom explains the emergence of a 'creolised' population, neither Black nor White, but culturally close to Europe and European ways. This new class caused problems in its relations not only with the Black slaves but with the colonial authorities. Occasionally children born of such unions inherited considerable wealth through financial legacies, and in the 1760s the Jamaica House of Assembly passed regulations banning all bequests to the children of planters by slave women.

*

Plantations in the British West Indies differed from those in other territories in that, by the late 18th century, Britain was leading the way in production management and the organisation of large-scale enterprises in agriculture and industry. The plantation system established in the Caribbean was an expression of all those economic developments. It was unique to modern agriculture in combining industrial production with agricultural labour on a huge scale, though even in the 17th century the sugar mill had been the largest industrial complex known to modern agriculture.

Overall the deepest effects on the African psyche can be attributed fundamentally to the slave being owned by someone else, and it is this which is most actively discussed in today's Caribbean communities. Patrick Bryan, a Jamaican historian, says:

> *I think we should talk about it, I think we should talk about our history. We need to come to terms with it. If you see an illness you must identify the illness and try to treat it accordingly. There are, however, Jamaicans who think that we talk too much about slavery, that we should really forget it. I think that those are the guilty ones, those people who feel that they were beneficiaries of the system and, if you talk about it too much, you might cause Black people to become the 'combustible' people that everybody knows that we are. But those people who dare to tell me that I shouldn't talk about slavery, I really let them have it. The Jews talk about their holocaust and*

I don't see why we shouldn't. And I think that most Jamaicans are willing to talk about it. I don't think that they hold it back.

It is the people who refuse to discuss it who constitute the problem.

FINANCE &
ECONOMICS

Standing on the terrace of his garden in Clifton, the entrepreneur Thomas Goldney could enjoy one of the most gratifying vistas in 18th-century England. He was surrounded by signs of his success. Out to the horizon he could see the busy traffic in Bristol harbour. There were ships coming in from North America and the West Indies laden with sugar, rum, tobacco and cotton and there were slave-ships going out to West Africa, their holds packed with brass, copper, glassware and wool. Other ships were making a shorter journey, bringing commodities from Shropshire to trade around the Bristol Channel area. Goldney had interests in all these activities.

His immediate environment, too, was a reminder of his connections with the wider world. Within his immaculately laid-out gardens stood an ornate tower which housed a steam pump of the type used to pump out mines. This machine, produced by his own Coalbrookdale Company in Shropshire, was customised to recycle water backwards and forwards to irigate his estate, in the same way that the Shropshire ironmasters powered their blast furnaces. Running directly beneath the terrace was a tunnel which led to a lavishly decorated grotto full of shells from Africa and the West Indies. These decorations had been presented to Goldney by his friend and former colleague, the slave-trader Captain Woodes Rogers. Pride of place in this underground chamber went to two great clam shells from the South Seas. At one end of the grotto stood a great statue, out of which water gushed, and on the floor was another key to his pioneering industrial exploits: the terracotta floor tiles had been specially made at great cost in Shropshire at the Horse Hay Works, using a new method of production. They cost over £30 to lay.

At the outset of his commercial career Goldney had been variously described as a grocer, a 'scavenger', and a warehouseman. Clifton-born and bred, he was an investor in a privateering voyage of Woodes Rogers in the early 18th century. This voyage made a fortune and the capital enabled Goldney to invest in a number of industrial enterprises in Bristol, the Avon Valley and Shropshire which established the merchant dynasty that continued until the later part of the century. His son, also Thomas, carried on and was one of the major partners in the development of the industrial revolution in the mid-18th century. What then was the secret of Thomas Goldney's rise to industrial eminence and how does that tie in with the fortunes of Bristol itself?

BRISTOL

By 1698 Bristol merchants of all varieties were already enjoying great profits from the market in human beings. One of the most successful entrepreneurs, John Cary, extolled the triangular trade as:

*A trade of the most advantage to this kingdom of any
we drive, and as it were all profit, the first cost being
little more than small matters of our own manufactures, for which we have in return, gold, elephants'
teeth, wax and negroes, the last whereof is much better
than the first, being indeed the best traffic the kingdom
hath, as it doth occasionally give so vast an employment to our people both by sea and land.*

With a cargo of 170 slaves the average Bristol voyage in the
1730s would have netted £8,000. It is estimated that between
1630 and 1807 two and a half million Africans had been bought
and sold by British slave merchants, netting them an overall
profit of £12 million. Bristol's most successful slave traders were
James Laroche, who financed 132 voyages between 1728 and
1769, James Day, who profited from 56 voyages between 1711
and 1742, and Isaac Hobhouse, who undertook 44 slave voyages
between 1722 and 1747.

The Goldneys' path to success was not unusual in this
booming port city. Merchants of all ranks traditionally took part
in trading ventures, as was noted by Roger North, an attorney-
general in the reign of James I:

*All men that are dealers, even in shop trades, launch
into adventures by sea, chiefly to the West India
plantations and Spain. A poor shopkeeper that sells
candles will have a bale of stockings or a piece of stuff
for Nevis or Virginia. And rather than fail, they trade
in men.*

Bristol in the early 1700s saw the development of a number of remarkable partnerships between people who had money and people who were able to exploit the latest manufacturing technologies. Thomas Goldney's relationship with his sometime partner Abraham Darby is an example. Darby had the technology and know-how, Goldney the money, obtained from the privateering voyages he had invested in a few years earlier. The combination brought about the brass industry in Bristol and the development of a string of brass and copper mills along the Avon. The river was fundamental. The water supply was harnessed to power the battery hammers which produced the artefacts; and ships could sail straight from the mills down to Bristol harbour, where the goods could be transferred from a small river vessel into the larger ships bound for West Africa.

Brass and copper were highly valued in West Africa. Since medieval times Africans had referred to copper as 'red gold'. It was often exchanged pound for pound with gold in commerce with trans-Saharan traders. With the onset of the European slaving era copper, in the form of buttons, bars, chains and cooking utensils, had become a currency by which slaves were sold. Bristol cashed in, and dominated the slave trade in the early 18th century, because it could mass-produce large quantities of copper products easily and cheaply. It was this new wealth, from slaves and the sugar they produced, that helped Bristol to its place as 'England's second city' at that time.

Bristol had always been a special seaport in Western Europe. Through the Middle Ages and beyond it had a reputation for swashbuckling mariners who would make pioneering voyages, first down the Atlantic coast and into the Mediterranean, later across the Atlantic looking for cod. Bristolians would claim they 'discovered the new world before Cabot or Columbus' and certainly showed them the way. In the

16th century they pioneered the sugar trade and set up their own mills and refineries. In the early 17th the region developed off-shoots of the tobacco industry, making clay pipes and importing tobacco from the New World. An infrastructure was, therefore, in place for Bristolians to be pioneers in the triangular trade. The critical ingredient, however, was copper. With the repeal of the Mines Royal Act in the late 17th century, people could make their own copper; copper was what Africans wanted most of all; and in no time Bristol had the set-up to crack the trade. It already had connections with the West Indies; now it had the copper to develop the trade with West Africa.

It was from the 'trade in men' that Bristol made its fortune. A short tour of the early 18th-century port shows how this burgeoning wealth worked its way through the city.

The docklands were at the heart of its business, and Princes Street, now a derelict hodge-podge of post-war planning disasters, was a microcosm of all activities tangential to the slave trade. Near the docks was a new crane put in by the Merchant Venturers, the official lobby of the overseas merchant interests in Bristol. Across from the warehouses rows of residential houses were being built by merchants such as Henry Tongue, Michael Becher and Robert Hollidge who had investments in slaving ships and associated trades. Further along lay the Africa Tavern, in which the spoils from privateers were often auctioned, and close to that stood the Assembly Rooms, which by the 1750s and '60s were a symbol of the city's growing refinement. This would be where the sons and daughters of these rough and ready merchants began their induction into a more genteel lifestyle of country dances and minuets. From there it was a short walk back to their Georgian homes in Queens Square. This part of town, developed in the 1720s; was one of the first provincial examples of urban regeneration of the period. It was financed and driven by people involved directly in the slave trade and there were at least eight families in the square – among them Captain Woodes Rogers – whose fortunes were built on commerce with Africa, the West Indies, Carolina and Virginia. As a result of the square's connections, it became the site of the first American consulate in England. At the same time that residents such as Henry Bright were shipping slaves from Angola to St. Kitts in decks no higher than 4ft 2in, they were also investing in the Theatre Royal and new private libraries and becoming patrons of banks. Queens Square still serves to reflect the strange mixture of brutality and gentility which was part and parcel of the triangular trade.

Of all the Queens Square houses the Elton Mansion was the biggest and grandest, standing out from the uniform facade of the rest of the buildings. Abraham Elton, founder of this dynasty, began working life as an apprentice to a mariner. In time he became a master mariner himself but clearly had a strong entrepreneurial flair and was declared a merchant in the 1680s. He started off in wool. By 1690 he was powerful and rich enough to be made a member of the Merchant Venturers and eight years later he was on their standing committee as well as a member of the Common Council of Bristol.

This period was to prove a turning point in Bristol's commercial history. In 1698 there was a strong petition from the city and its Merchant Venturers to overturn the monopoly of the Royal Africa Company, which had sole trading rights to the African coast. Abraham Elton was by then involved in the copper business, having set up the Conham copper works in

1694 (which had failed to get a commission to produce the coinage of the realm), and was looking for African outlets. Driven by the desire to acquire mineral rights he diversified into buying land, purchasing tracts in the Mendips which were to prove abundant sources of calamine and land in Nailsea and Tickenham to corner the regional market in coal. He became master of the Merchant Venturers in 1708, bought Clevedon Court, along with estates in Whitestaunton and Winford in 1709 and a year later was mayor of Bristol. By 1717 he was so wealthy that he was in a position to contribute £10,000 to the depleted coffers of King George I and, true to the tradition of political patronage, he was made a baronet. He stood as Member of Parliament for Bristol in 1722. He had three sons, likewise rich and successful, and by the first two decades of the 18th century the Elton family was a power to be reckoned with.

The port of Bristol had come to dominate much of Britain's trade with Africa and, as Julia Elton, Sir Abraham's direct descendant, points out, Abraham Elton was only too keen to develop his part in it:

> *I think a very crucial part of his expanding success was the ability to trade with Africa in what became known as the triangular trade. He was able to load ships with his goods; his copper and his glass. The ships went to the west coast of Africa, exchanged the goods for slaves, took the slaves on the infamous middle passage to the English colonies of Virginia and the West Indies, dropped off the load of slaves and then brought back to Bristol sugar, tobacco and other goods. If you're in shipping, and as a master mariner, of course, he was, Abraham Elton was very familiar with*

enormous risks involved. Not only are there risks with the natural hazards of wind and wave and weather, England was very often at war, so that you were at risk from enemies at sea, from pirates and corsairs, so that what he wanted to do was to minimise the risks, and I think the Africa trade was essential to that.

LIVERPOOL

Bristol continued slave trading until abolition, but in decreasing numbers in the late 18th and early 19th centuries. By that stage other commodities were needed, not just copper but manufactured goods – textiles, iron, leather and ceramics – and the northern ports, Liverpool in particular, were best able to furnish these. Bristol was a difficult harbour to develop. The Avon itself is a navigable waterway but the rise and fall of the tide are considerable and ships would often end up on the mud, making unloading hazardous. By the 1780s the ships were much larger, two out of every five British slavers were built in Liverpool and the port had become the largest slave-ship construction site in England. It had other advantages. Duty could be evaded by storing goods on the Isle of Man. Liverpool was also notorious for outrageous cost-cutting practices. Young boys and inexperienced hands would be employed in preference to able seamen. Officers and crew were paid on an annual rather than a monthly basis, and agents were permitted only a five per cent commission on transactions. Effectively Bristol was squeezed out of the trade by the bigger more profitable ships from Liverpool that could operate on lower costs.

Liverpool's other speciality was to create a successful, though illegal, trade in slaves to the Spanish Empire. The city expanded spectacularly. As was the case in Bristol, business people of all stripes invested in the slave trade. J. Wallace, a Liverpool historian, wrote in 1795:

> *Almost every man in Liverpool is a merchant and he who cannot send a bale will send a bandbox. The attractive African meteor has so dazzled their ideas that almost every order of people is interested in a Guinea cargo. It is well known that many of the small vessels that import about a hundred slaves are fitted out by attorneys, drapers, ropers, grocers, tallow-chandlers, barbers, taylors etc, some have one-eighth, some a fifteenth [sic], and some a thirty-second.*

The first recorded slave voyage from Liverpool was in 1700. The ship was the *Liverpool Merchant* which transported 220 slaves to of Barbados. Following the success of that venture the slave trade came to the attention of the city's elders who threw themselves into it with greater abandon even than their counterparts in Bristol. Huge fortunes, which would later become the building blocks of banks and manufacturing interests, had their origins in the Liverpool slave trade. The Heywood brothers, Arthur and Benjamin, made their fortunes in the slave trade. The bank they founded on their profits, Arthur Heywood Sons & Co., would be absorbed in turn by the Bank of Liverpool, Martin's Bank and Barclay's Bank. Another high-street bank with connections to the slave trade can be traced back to the launch of Thomas Leyland's banking house in 1807. Leyland was one of the three richest men in Liverpool. Between 1782 to 1807 he shipped almost 3,500 slaves to Jamaica alone. He served as Mayor of Liverpool in 1798, 1814 and 1820. In 1901

Leyland and Bullin's Bank would become part of the North and South Wales Bank, which in turn was to be absorbed into the Midland Bank in 1908. Several other Liverpool mayors and Members of Parliament also had their fingers in the slave-trade pie. Thomas Johnson, a slaver since 1703, was an MP from 1701 to 1723. His son-in-law Richard Gildart and cousin James Gildart were, between them, mayors of Liverpool on five occasions from 1714 to 1750.

The Tarletons were a stereotypical Liverpool slave-trading family. The dynasty started with Thomas Tarleton, a slaver as early as 1720 whose son John established the family as leading figures in the city's slave-trading community. He was mayor in 1764 and died leaving a personal fortune of £80,000 and four sons: John, Clayton, Thomas and Banastre. John, Clayton and Thomas went into partnership with another slaver Daniel Backhouse and are quoted as supplying Spanish colonists with 3,000 slaves a year. Banastre was not involved directly in the trade but, as MP for Liverpool (1790-1806), spoke out in its favour. He eventually lost his seat to an abolitionist, although he was re-elected a year later. Meanwhile Clayton had been mayor in 1792. A plaque commemorating Banastre Tarleton's birth still stands in Fenwick Street and until the 1920s the family owned a plantation in Grenada called Carria Cou. Christopher Tarleton Fagan, a living descendant, sees his family's connection with slavery like this:

> They traded in many things, and with the growth of the sugar plantations in the West Indies, labour was required. The labour was found from slaves in West Africa, the slaves being sold by the Africans them-

selves. It was part of the trade which was carried out in the context of that age. Today, quite clearly, slavery is completely abhorrent and unjustified. But I think one's got to remember that slavery has been going on since time immemorial. It was widespread throughout the world and it was not considered to be an appalling thing to be involved in in those days.

One family clearly unappalled at the time were the famous Gladstones of Liverpool. John Gladstones owned sugar plantations in British Guyana and Jamaica. When not trading with the colonies, India, China and Russia, he wrote as a renowned pro-slavery columnist for the *Liverpool Mercury* under the name of Mercator. It goes without saying that he was the city's Member of Parliament (1818-1827). The Gladstones family dropped the final 's' from their name in 1835 after John's son, William Ewart, the future Liberal Prime Minister, had entered the House of Commons as MP for Newark in 1832.

LONDON

Although London would be eclipsed by Bristol and Liverpool as a slave-trading port, its involvement in the trade was both longer and deeper than that of the other two cities.

The capital, up until 1698, had enjoyed the commercial privileges bestowed on it by the charter of the Royal Africa Company, and the City and its officials had grown fat on its revenues. Under this monopoly 100,000 Africans had been shipped to the colonies and 30,000 tons of sugar had been imported. No fewer than 15 Lord Mayors, 25 sheriffs and 38 aldermen of the City of London were shareholders in the company between 1660 and 1690. Following its decline as a slaving port, London assumed a more permanent and central role as the financial hub of the triangular trade. Given the risky and long-term nature of a typical slave voyage, new forms of credit were introduced into the British banking system. The need for long-term credit, with bills payable after anything from one and a half to three years, led to the development of specialist banking houses such as that operated by Alexander and David Barclay, whose bank bears the family name to this day. Even more active in this field was Sir Francis Baring, who was reputed to have made his initial fortune as a 16-year-old slave dealer. Baring was to sit as a member of parliament for 18 years and died leaving a legacy valued at £1,000,000.

The Bank of England itself was also to figure largely in this enterprise. Sir Richard Neave, the bank's director for 48 years, also sat as chairman of the Society of West India Merchants. Neave's son-in-law, Beeston Long, would follow in his footsteps both as chairman of the Merchants and governor of the Bank of England. Pulling the strings of all parties in this business was the enormously influential body of planters and their representatives who sat in the House of Commons. A contributor to the *Gentleman's Magazine* in 1766 estimated:

> . . . *there are now in parliament upwards of forty members who are either West India planters them- selves, descended from such or have concerns there that entitle them to this pre-eminence.*

Given such an unprecedented concentration of political and economic power, it was inevitable that the plantation system would produce England's first millionaire: William Beckford MP. The Beckford family typified the style of 'old corruption' politics by which rotten and pocket boroughs could be bought outright. The owner of more than 22,000 acres in Jamaica, William Beckford sat as the Member of Parliament for Shaftesbury from 1747-54 and for London itself from 1754-70. His brother Richard sat for Bristol and his second brother Julines for Salisbury. His son Richard would serve as Member of Parliament for Bridport, Arundel and Leominster. His other son William, an eccentric author, collector, composer and landscape gardener, would sit for Wells and later for Hindon. William Beckford Junior would build up, over his lifetime, a collection of 20,000 books, furniture, objets d'art and paintings by Bronzino, Titian, Rubens, Velasquez, Caneletto and Raphael. He would house it all in Fonthill Abbey in Wiltshire, a country mansion the size of a cathedral, which had been designed for him by James Wyatt. Fonthill Abbey was the original gothic monstrosity: the tower of the Great Octagon soared upwards for 300 feet and was so fantastically perpendicular that it collapsed several times, the final time in 1825 due to improper foundations. To complete the effect, he hired a dwarf to open the 38-foot-high front doors. Lord Byron described him as 'England's wealthiest son'.

The influence of the merchants involved in the Africa and Atlantic trades was asserted, in the first instance, through their power to found banks and dominate the financial institutions of London, as well as the provinces as they became more estab-lished. In due course, though, their connections with land-owning families multiplied and they built stately homes and acquired political influence. Often they had started off outside the mainstream of national life, perhaps as supporters of Nonconformist churches. But, as they waxed more prosperous and married in to the aristocracy, they were able to buy rotten

boroughs. It was a commercial transaction for political influence
– seats in the House of Commons. Nominally they represented a
town or borough in Britain but there were only two or three
electors. The upshot was 50 or 60 MPs representing the slave
plantations.

Thus was their power and this was how they achieved it:
by the end of the 18th century there were around a million slaves
in the British Caribbean working about 3,000 hours a year
unrecompensed, growing their own food largely in their own
very scant spare time. This is 3,000 million hours' free labour
producing sugar, coffee and cotton. And the population of
England at the time was only five million.

A visitor to the site of William Beckford's Fonthill Abbey in 1823
declared: 'Would to God it was more substantially built! But as it
is, its ruins will tell a tale of wonder!'

In March 1999, Robert Beckford, a Black British man,
surveying the Abbey's north wing, was not so sure.

> *Well, it is an amazing piece of restoration and it looks*
> *fantastic. But there's something missing. This is part*
> *of English heritage, but they're not telling the full*
> *story. There isn't anything within the building or*
> *anything within the restoration that deals with the*
> *slave past and the fact that this was a slave-holding*
> *family who took millions of pounds from slaves in the*
> *plantations in Jamaica. So how can this really be*
> *English heritage? It's really a partial and myopic view*
> *of English heritage.*
>
> *Beckford was obviously a man with a great*
> *deal of money and a great deal of time to cultivate fine*

tastes. But again he removes himself from this plantation past and engages in a kind of historical amnesia which I think is being reproduced here today.

I think William Beckford personifies the whole period of slavery. People lived well, ate well, were able to cultivate taste in art, and in other artefacts, but yet they didn't pay any attention to where the money came from; that was almost a distant thing happening somewhere else in the world. And it symbolises a view of the world in which you can live well and build these fantastic monuments, but you don't have to remember too much about where the money came from. As a consequence you don't have to tell the full story. It's almost a dishonest history.

PART THREE

RESISTANCE

ABOLITION

The idea that human beings, White or Black, can be reduced to chattel labour goes back to antiquity. The Bible offers us the story of 'the sons of Ham', who were cursed with perpetual bondage because Ham had seen 'his father's nakedness', and both Christians and Muslims adopted this Judaic justification for slavery, accepting the suggestion of a hereditary taint according to which entire nations and races might be enslaved. So how did this trade come to be seen as unacceptable?

The second half of the 18th century saw a growth of sentimental art and literature in which Black people were seen not necessarily as equal to Whites but as fellow human beings with bodies that can suffer and souls that can be saved. The initial concern of those religious people committed to abolitionism was not so much for the freedom of the bodies of slaves but for their souls. This may seem a bizarre priority now but at the time, in a deeply religious society, the perspective was crucial. That Black people were condemned to servitude was seen as secondary to the eternal damnation of their souls.

The individual who, more than anyone, embodied this

'change of heart' in his own lifetime was the slaver-turned-clergyman John Newton. At the church of St Mary Woolnoth in London's Lombard Street the details of his conversion are inscribed on a memorial. Newton was born in the 1720s, the son of a merchant seaman. Having set out in the same business as his father, he became a 'servant' to slave traders in Africa (some of whom, the memorial points out, were Black). As a slaver himself, he captained the *Duke of Argyll* and the *African* but in 1748 he underwent a religious conversion and twelve years later was rector at St Mary's. He wrote the hymn 'How Sweet the Name of Jesus Sounds' and became an impassioned preacher and writer on the slave trade, offering his own life as an example of a conversion process which the nation at large should follow.

Not all organised religion's connections with the slave trade were as clear-cut or poetically just as John Newton's. Many sections of Christian society believed it was possible to treat slaves well while denying them civil liberties. In 18th-century Barbados, for example, the Bishops of London owned and operated the plantations from which Codrington College was eventually established. Profits generated from the plantations came back to England and directly financed churches here, as records at Lambeth Palace attest. The estate was managed for over 150 years and at the height of slavery on the island in the 1780s the Church of England was in the vanguard of slave owning. The leading slave owner was, in fact, an Anglican clergyman, the Reverend John Braithwaite. He owned more than six estates and almost 2,000 slaves.

The official church of Jamaica was the Anglican Church, to which most planters subscribed. It was commonly held that to teach slaves Christianity would be to barbarise the Gospel;

besides, teaching oppressed people Christian virtues might lead them to think in terms of their own freedom. As a result Blacks were generally not permitted to attend services. Even though the Anglican Church in England had favoured the conversion of slaves to Christianity since 1696, the local Anglican establishment did not take this approach until well over a century later, and then only in a customised manner. Slaves could be taught industry, thrift and obedience and be introduced to selected passages of Scripture, such as Ecclesiastes 8:6: 'Whoever obeys a command will meet no harm;' or from the same book, 10:20: 'Curse not the king, even in your thoughts, or curse the rich, even in your bedroom; or a bird of the air may carry your voice, or some winged creature tell the matter.' Such preachers seem not to have realised that the slaves had minds of their own and would interpret the gospel as they thought fit, in terms of their own ideology of freedom. The most telling example of this use of Scripture came from the Black Baptist preacher and activist Sam Sharpe, whose rallying cry was: 'No man can serve two masters.'

Marginalisation at least gave the slaves room to practise their own traditions, which allowed the continuation of African culture.

Things began to change in the mid-18th century with the coming of Nonconformist religious sects, such as the Moravians, Baptists, Quakers and Methodists. Back in Britain the Nonconformists, having broken away from the Church of England, had sparked off a religious revival, and now it was spreading on both sides of the Atlantic.

Not surprisingly the Quakers, alienated from the state and with their roots in 17th-century radicalism, were prominent in the abolitionist battle. Large numbers of Quaker families had made their fortunes in the triangular trade, so there may have been an extra element of assuaging their sense of guilt. The Quakers gave lecture-tours in which they spoke out against the evils of slavery. They made a special point of visiting well-established schools such as Eton, Harrow, Westminster, Charterhouse, Winchester and St Paul's. When the Society for the Abolition of the Slave Trade was formed in 1787, nine out of its twelve committee members were Quakers.

The Methodists, while also promoting good works above faith alone as the route to salvation, had more traditional allegiances and concerned themselves with the eternal souls of both masters and slaves, as in this passionate appeal from John Wesley:

> *Thou who hast mingled of one blood all the nations upon earth: Have compassion upon those outcasts of men, who are trodden down as dung upon the earth. Arise and help these that have no helper, whose blood is spilt upon the ground like water! Are not these also the work of thine hands, the purchase of thy Son's blood? Stir them up to cry unto thee in the land of their captivity; and let their complaint come up before thee; let it enter into thine ears! Make even those that lead them away captive to pity them, and turn their captivity as the rivers of the South. O burst thou all their chains in sunder; more especially the chains of their sins: Thou, O Saviour of all, make them free, that they may be free indeed!*

Methodist fervour aside, however, the campaign for abolition triumphed not just because it appealed to deeply religious people and intellectuals. There had long been stirrings against slavery, even in establishment circles. As early as 1750 there were *private* expressions of disgust at parliamentary level, such as this from the MP Horace Walpole:

> *We have been sitting this fortnight on the Africa Company, we, the British Senate, that temple of liberty, bulwark of Protestant Christianity, have this fortnight been pondering methods to make more effectual that horrid traffic of selling negroes. It has appeared to us that six-and-forty thousand of these wretches are to be sold every year to our plantations alone! – it chills one's blood. I would not want to say I voted for it for the continent of America.*

In the end accepting the abolitionist cause suited the British establishment in several ways, with an appeal to patriotism always at the heart of it. By 1800 Britain was so prosperous that its rulers increasingly felt they could withdraw from the slave trade without too much economic damage. The parliamentary position, in all its ambivalence and unsentimentality, was well expressed in Henry Brougham's 1803 *Inquiry into the Colonial Policy of the European Powers*:

> *. . . the fruit of our iniquity has been a great and rich empire in America. Let us be satisfied with our gains and, being rich, let us try to become righteous – not indeed by giving up a single sugar cane of what we have acquired but by continuing in our present state of overflowing opulence and preventing the further importation of slaves . . . The experience of the United*

*States has distinctly proved that the rapid multi-
plication of the Blacks in a natural way will inevitably
be occasioned by prohibiting their importation . . . the
structure of West Indian society will more and more
resemble that of the compact, firm and respectable
communities which compose the North American
states.*

And, with an eye firmly fixed on Toussaint L'Ouverture's rebellion in Haiti twelve years earlier, he added:

*When a fire is raging windward, is it the proper time
for stirring up everything that is combustible in your
warehouse and throwing into them new loads of
material still more prone to explosion? Surely, surely,
these most obvious considerations only have to be
hinted at to demonstrate that, independent of any
other considerations against the negro traffic, the
present state of the French West Indies renders the
idea of continuing its existence for another hour worse
than infamy.*

From the establishment point of view abolition was also timely.
Having recently lost a war in North America and finding itself
deeply involved in a war with revolutionary France, Britain was
fighting not just for survival but to establish its credentials as a
great nation. Thanks to the anti-slavery movement, Britons
could stand up in 1807 (when British participation in the slave
trade was abolished) and proclaim that they were better than the
slave-owning 'libertarians' in America and the slave-owning
French with whom they were at war. Or, cynically, anti-slavery

had an appeal not just to reformers but to orthodox patriots who saw in it one more proof that Britain was the supreme land of liberty.

Even in the land of liberty any battle against interests as powerful and entrenched as the West India lobby was sure to prove tough. The planters and merchants put up a long rearguard defence of slavery but there were strong forces ranged against them.

By the end of the 18th century slavery had become a symbol of 'old corruption'. It posed a revolutionary challenge to the distribution of power in the country. Many of the older landed families saw the West India merchants as *nouveau-riche* upstarts who had far too much political leverage whereas sectors of the British economy (in Yorkshire, for example), which were less involved in the colonial system, were more comfortable with an abolitionist MP like William Wilberforce. His family were wool merchants, who might have regarded cotton as a rival interest.

The movement for abolition gained its greatest impetus at a more popular level. People began to realise with revulsion the dimensions of this trade and its human cost. Not only Africans died on the Middle Passage, though it was bad enough that well over a million slaves perished during the Atlantic crossings of the 18th century. Anti-slavery campaigners were appalled that British seamen were dying at an even higher comparative rate. Whatever the motivations, the major engines of abolition lay well beyond the walls of Parliament and centred on the classes who had profited least from it.

The figures speak for themselves. In 1792 500 anti-slavery petitions were presented to Parliament; by the 1830s that figure had risen to 5,000. Between 1826 and 1832 the House of Lords received over 3,500 petitions. For the British working classes slavery was an embodiment of the worst aspects of a system under which they themselves were largely disenfranchised. As the radical John Thelwall expressed it in 1795:

> *The seed, the root of the oppression is here; and here the*
> *cure must begin ... If we would dispense justice to our*
> *distant colonies, we must begin by rooting out from*
> *the centre the corruption by which that cruelty and*
> *injustice is countenanced and defended.*

Great Britain by the early 1830s had become the scene of wide-scale discontent. New working-class organisations were emerging, like the Union of the Working Classes which drew a crowd in excess of 70,000 to a demonstration in London in October 1831. The 'Captain Swing' riots, in which agricultural labourers rose up against their rich landlords, blazed through the English countryside during the same period. Throughout the country, political unions were formed to demand universal male suffrage and the abolition of the 'rotten borough' system. Marching and drilling were the most ominous signs of this new body of opinion.

At roughly the same time, Christmas 1831, was the slave uprising in Jamaica known as Sam Sharpe's Revolt. More than 400 slaves were killed in repressing the revolt but its most visible effect in England was the presence of half a dozen British Nonconformist ministers who had been beaten, tarred and feathered, jailed and finally deported from Jamaica for their supposed involvement. This inflamed opinion in Britain against the slave owners and an armed and organised working class firmly

A typical mid-18th-century British trading vessel, the Jason Privateer.
Many such ships transported slaves to Africa, carrying around 170 slaves on
each voyage. The panels show European traders buying slaves.

A convoy of Africans being driven by their captors to the coast
to be sold to European traders.

An 18th-century illustration of a slave fort on the west coast of Africa. In the top half African fishermen go about their work close to the slave ships. In the bottom half slaves are transported to a slave ship to begin their journey to the West Indies.

The middle passage. Slaves were crammed into the ships' holds for weeks on end, with barely enough food, drink and air to keep them alive. Many did not survive the journey.

Having arrived in the West Indies, the slaves were often sold to plantation owners by public auction. Those deemed unfit for sale were classed as 'refuse' and left to perish in the docks.

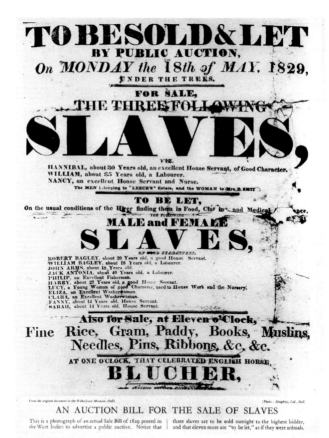

TO BE SOLD & LET
BY PUBLIC AUCTION,
On MONDAY the 18th of MAY, 1829,
UNDER THE TREES.
FOR SALE,
THE THREE FOLLOWING
SLAVES,
VIZ.

HANNIBAL, about 30 Years old, an excellent House Servant, of Good Character.
WILLIAM, about 35 Years old, a Labourer.
NANCY, an excellent House Servant and Nurse.

The MEN belonging to "LEECH'S" Estate, and the WOMAN to Mrs. D. SMIT

TO BE LET,
On the usual conditions of the Hirer finding them in Food, Clothing and Medical Assistance,
THE FOLLOWING
MALE and FEMALE
SLAVES,
OF GOOD CHARACTERS,

ROBERT BAGLEY, about 20 Years old, a good House Servant.
WILLIAM BAGLEY, about 18 Years old, a Labourer.
JOHN ARMS, about 18 Years old.
JACK ANTONIA, about 40 Years old, a Labourer.
PHILIP, an Excellent Fisherman.
HARRY, about 27 Years old, a good House Servant.
LUCY, a Young Woman of good Character, used to House Work and the Nursery.
ELIZA, an Excellent Washerwoman.
CLARA, an Excellent Washerwoman.
FANNY, about 14 Years old, House Servant.
SARAH, about 14 Years old, House Servant.

Also for Sale, at Eleven o'Clock,
Fine Rice, Gram, Paddy, Books, Muslins, Needles, Pins, Ribbons, &c. &c.
AT ONE O'CLOCK, THAT CELEBRATED ENGLISH HORSE,
BLUCHER,

From the original document in the Wilberforce Museum, Hull]   *[Photo : Doughtys, Ltd., Hull*

AN AUCTION BILL FOR THE SALE OF SLAVES

This is a photograph of an actual Sale Bill of 1829 posted in the West Indies to advertise a public auction. Notice that three slaves are to be sold outright to the highest bidder, and that eleven more are "to be let," as if they were animals.

Slaves tilling a field on a plantation in Antigua, 1790.

Discipline at the plantations was maintained through brutal punishment and even execution. Here one slave metes out punishment to another.

Bristol docks, 1750, a thriving port grown rich on the triangular trade.

Hogarth's Marriage à la Mode, *1745. Black servants were seen as exotic and fashionable additions to wealthy British households.*

Abolitionist Granville Sharp, here portrayed trying to prevent a slave captain from taking an escaped slave back into captivity.

The abolitionists' emblem. This powerful image was reproduced on many domestic artefacts including glassware, crockery, needlework, coins and figurines.

Olaudah Equiano, writer, orator and abolitionist. His first-hand account of enslavement had a powerful impact on the British public.

A rebel slave. The disruption caused by slave revolts on the plantations played a pivotal role in bringing an end to slavery.

The growing black population of London was represented in contemporary images of domestic life, such as this caricature of kitchen staff from 1810.

An illustration of Miss Swartz from the Victorian novel Vanity Fair. This crude representation reflects the negative portrayal of this mixed-race character in the novel.

British naval vessels attacking a slave-trading establishment in Mozambique, 1851.

MONKEYANA.

AM I satyr or man ?
Pray tell me who can,
And settle my place in the scale.
A man in ape's shape,
An anthropoid ape,
Or monkey deprived of his tail ?

Twenty-seven years after abolition, the abolitionists' motto is parodied in this
Punch *magazine cartoon, which reflects upon the new theory of evolution,*
revealing the scientific racism that it spawned.

behind abolition gave many in the aristocracy cause for concern. According to one member of the House of Lords:

> *The idea of abolishing the slave trade is connected with the levelling system and the rights of man . . . What does the abolition of the slave trade mean more or less in effect, than liberty and equality? What more or less than the rights of man? And what is liberty and equality, and what the rights of man, but the foolish fundamental principles of this new philosophy. If proofs are wanting, look at the colony of Santo Domingo [Haiti] and see what the rights of man have done there.*

If striking down slavery became the first item on the agenda of reform, other inhuman economic practices that were enriching only a minority and threatening the health and conditions of life of the majority would be next. Abolition of slavery was seen as merely the *first* instalment of social reform.

This heady mix of radicalism, evangelism and political opportunism produced three outstanding characters who were, in their own necessarily muted ways, masters of all three disciplines. William Wilberforce, as MP for Hull, was the most public face and therefore best remembered of the reformers. As a Member of Parliament he was the most conservative of the three – a quality which his conversion to evangelical Christianity in 1785 did nothing to alter. In 1807, following the passage of the act suppressing slavery, the call went up from a young MP for a bill demanding the gradual emancipation of all slaves in the British colonies. Wilberforce was strongly against this, stating that, even though he anticipated a time when Blacks might 'with safety be liberated', he felt they were not yet 'fit . . . to bear emancipation'. Like many non-working-class abolitionists, he believed the ending of the traffic in human cargoes would lead to an improvement in the slaves' living conditions as a result of market forces and Christian values.

In May 1787 Wilberforce met Thomas Clarkson, England's most courageous agitator against the slave trade. One year Wilberforce's junior, and like him a graduate of Cambridge, Clarkson was an altogether different breed of activist. The son of a headmaster, Clarkson had published three years earlier *An Essay on the Slavery and Commerce of the Human Species*. The work he now undertook, of gathering information about the excesses of the trade, carried him all over the country. Of his approach to Bristol he wrote that he 'began now to tremble at the arduous task' and realised he was 'attempting to subvert one of the branches of the commerce of the great place which was then before me'. In Bristol and Liverpool he set about interviewing city officials as well as the captains and crew, both active and retired, of slaving vessels. Occasionally he met with violence but the presence of a bodyguard saved him from any great personal injury.

With Wilberforce as parliamentary figurehead, the Committee for Effecting the Abolition of the Slave Trade was set up in 1787. Within a year, mostly as a result of Clarkson's activities, a Privy Council committee was formed to look into the trade. In 1791 Clarkson travelled 7,000 miles and recorded visits to 320 ships. This same year saw the introduction in the House of Commons of Wilberforce's motion to abolish slavery. After a two-day debate the motion was defeated by 163 votes to 88. An amended version of this bill, which asked for 'gradual' abolition, was passed in the Commons by 230 votes to 85 in the following year. Inevitably it met great opposition in the House of Lords, where it was postponed for a year and left to gather dust.

Preceding both Clarkson and Wilberforce was Granville Sharp, who can safely claim the title of Britain's first anti-slavery campaigner. Coming from a wealthy and deeply religious family – his father was an archdeacon, his grandfather Archbishop of York – Granville Sharp's role in the anti-slavery movement was to be played out almost entirely away from the parliamentary arena.

It was while working as a clerk in the Ordnance Office in 1765 that he took up the case of Jonathan Strong, a runaway slave he had found on the streets of London and helped to escape the clutches of his master. In 1769 he published his first pamphlet, *A Representation of the Injustice and Dangerous Tendency of Tolerating Slavery; or of Admitting the Least Claim of Private Property in the Persons of Men, in England.* His success in the Strong case led him to take on others involving London's Black poor, most notably that of James Somerset in 1771.

Somerset was a slave who faced the prospect of abduction from London back to the colonies. In the face of considerable opposition lined up on the side of Somerset's master, Sharp, aided by radicals and London Blacks, succeeded in bringing the case before the Chief Justice, Lord Mansfield. Eventually, after much to-ing and fro-ing, Mansfield made the historic ruling which forbade a slave owner to deport his slave to the colonies from English soil: 'The state of slavery is of such a nature that it is incapable of being now introduced by justice upon mere reasoning.' Though this was widely misinterpreted as bestowing liberty on all slaves in England, it was still a major blow to the slave-owning lobby – a public denial of positive support from high authority in the judiciary.

One area where support for the planters was guaranteed was inside the royal family. Always ardent champions of slavery, the monarchy had been a thorn in the reformers' side since the first motion in 1791. Obviously the Lords and Commons were familiar with the royal point of view and nothing had changed by 1806 when Wilberforce, readying himself for fresh lobbying in the coming parliamentary session, remarked: 'The great point would be to get, if possible, the royal family to give up their position.'

Because of fears that the King would use the royal veto to block the measure, what became the Foreign Slave Trade Bill, introduced in April 1806, merely forbade British traders to sell slaves to foreign territories. Throughout its drafting abolitionists stayed in the background and the House of Lords accepted the bill by 43 votes to 18. Emboldened by this success, the abolitionists then pressed ahead with all speed. An amended bill, which included their central demand, the suppression of the slave trade, was passed by the Lords in 1807. This time the vote was 100 to 36. It was passed in the Commons by 283 votes to 16. Under this legislation British involvement in slave trading between the west coast of Africa and the Americas was to end by the first day of 1808.

Taking a sceptical view of the whole issue of parliamentary involvement, the historian Dr Hakim Adi has this to say:

> Abolition did have the effect of aiding Britain's war effort, and it has to be remembered that before the abolition of the slave trade in 1807 there was an Act in

1806 which prohibited the export of slaves to Britain's foreign rivals, and it was very much presented at the time as being in the national interest. This was a law which enabled Britain to outdo and undermine its competitors. So we shouldn't think of the abolition of the slave trade in 1807 simply as a humanitarian gesture. We shouldn't think that in the nineteenth century the government of Britain, the commercial interests in Britain, suddenly realised the error of their ways and said, okay, we were the greatest slave traders in the eighteenth century, but now we're going to be the greatest abolitionists. It wasn't quite as straightforward as that. One thing that has to be born in mind is that Britain's economic position was changing as well, that Britain in the early part of the nineteenth century, but much more by the mid-nineteenth century, was becoming the workshop of the world, the pre-eminent manufacturing power, industrial power and so on. So its commercial and economic interests were changing. At the same time, it's been argued that the plantation economies of the Caribbean were becoming less important.

The British government certainly did want to present itself in the nineteenth century as the great humanitarian power which intervened all over the world for humanitarian reasons. The same is true today – that the British government presents itself as being concerned – for example, in Yugoslavia – with humanitarianism and so on. But I think that, if one looks further, it's easy to see that the British government – or certainly those interests it represents – have various other concerns, whether they're economic, political or strategic, which are masked by this humanitarianism, and that was certainly the case in the nineteenth century. What British government was particularly concerned about was British trade, Britain's economy and the fact that Britain was an imperial world power. Those were the chief concerns. If humanitarianism furthered those interests, then fine. If it had gotten in the way of those interests, then it would have been largely ignored.

Whatever the benefits to the nation, the abolitionists had achieved their victory, and it had not been an easy one. For moderate reformers, abolition of the slave trade was the end of the road. For other participants, more radical and newly politicised, it was just a step on the road. Ending the slave trade did not mean the ending of slavery. There remained greater goals to fight for: emancipation (the freeing of the slaves still held in captivity) and wholesale parliamentary change.

BLACK REVOLT AND BLACK RADICALS

In 1752 the *Marlborough*, a Bristol ship owned by Walter Lougher and Co. and manned by a crew of 35, set off across the Atlantic with a cargo of 400 slaves from Bonny and the Gold Coast. A few days later 28 Gold Coast men found themselves on deck while the sailors were occupied in cleaning the slaves' quarters below. Somehow they had seized a number of muskets and killed all but eight of the crew. These eight, on the orders of their new masters, sailed the ship back to Bonny. On reaching the coast the *Marlborough* came under attack from the *Hawk*, another Bristol slaver, but the ex-slaves had quickly mastered the use of firearms and put the *Hawk* to flight.

The story, however, had a messy ending. The two groups of Africans began to quarrel among themselves and soon came to blows. Those from the Gold Coast came out victorious but only at the cost of a hundred lives. The survivors of this slaughter eventually made their way back to their respective homes.

The story of abolition has often been told from the viewpoint of British parliamentarians and agitators. What they thought and did was important but Black captives in African slave ports and the New World could not afford to wait for new philosophies or the vagaries of parliamentary reform to move in their favour. They acted and their actions counted. Slave rebellions had an impact on the reform process, as did the work of Black radicals based in London.

The history of slavery is as much one of rebellion as of enforced servitude. For more than 300 years slave rebellions and White fears about them were central factors of colonial life. The greatest fear was the prospect of large groups of armed runaways taking over the interior of a colony and mounting raids on plantations and White settlements. By the early 18th century large communities of fugitive slaves had established themselves through Argentina, Brazil, Surinam, Guyana, Venezuela and New Granada (present day Colombia). The experience of those Latin American colonies served as a constant reminder to territories under British rule of what might happen.

But, as the case of the *Marlborough* demonstrated, rebellion and resistance were not confined to the plantations. Uprisings could be expected at any point on the Atlantic crossing. The majority took place while the ships lay off the African coast or were preparing to disembark. It is estimated that an insurrection occurred every eight to ten journeys. Most were quashed rapidly and with extreme severity.

A typical story is that of the *Robert* in 1760, where a

handful of slaves tried '. . . to kill the ship's company and attempt their escapes, while they had a shore to fly to, and had near effected it by means of a woman-slave who, being more at large, was to watch the proper opportunity'. The 'proper opportunity' came one night when the conspirators were alerted that there were only five White men on deck. The slaves' ringleader, with only a hammer, the slave-woman and another male slave to aid him, managed to kill two sleeping seamen. It was to no avail. The commotion had woken up the rest of the crew, including the ship's master Captain Harding, who '. . . took a handspike, the first thing he met with in the surprise, and, redoubling his strokes upon Tomba [the ringleader], laid him at length flat upon the deck, securing them all in irons . . .' Gruesome retribution followed: whippings, hoistings by the thumbs, mutilation and the enforced cannibalism of co-conspirators.

Stories like this were soon being reported in the English-language press. They fuelled a growing myth concerning Black violence, treachery and sullenness and, ultimately, the myth was used to justify the harsh methods needed to contain such insurrection. The *Newport Mercury* reported in 1765:

> . . . the brig Sally . . . *arrived here in Antigua from the coast of Africa, we learn that soon after he left the coast, the number of his men being reduced by sickness, he was obliged to permit some of the slaves to come upon deck to assist the people: these slaves contrived to release the others, and the whole rose upon the people and endeavoured to get possession of the vessel; but was happily prevented by the captain, who killed, wounded and forced overboard eighty of them which obliged the rest to submit.*

The most extreme violence (and propaganda) was reserved for use against uprisings on the plantations themselves, where the damage to European lives, property and pride was greater. In the 18th and 19th centuries the New World colonies experienced a major slave rebellion every 20 years or so. Added to these were countless minor attempts at insurrection, resistance and sabotage. Conflict was the norm and the West Indian colonies were, to one degree or another, in a perpetual state of civil war. Every uprising on the plantation had its roots in the dehumanised conditions of slave life but two of the most far-reaching were also the indirect result of changes sweeping in from outside.

SAM SHARPE'S REVOLT

Although virtually all White missionaries and their Black deacons preached submission to authority, the spread of Nonconformist Christianity through the West Indies served to speed the demise of the established order. Methodists, Baptists and Moravians had been active in Jamaica since the 1750s. Their teachings on forgiveness and obedience had originally been welcomed by the planters, most of whom belonged to the expressly White Church of England. Seventy years later Jamaican Nonconformist congregations numbered 8,000 strong. While the White community adhered to Anglicanism, Nonconformism soon became a focus for Black self-expression. Services were conducted in patois. Bible classes were held. Reading, if only of the Scriptures, was occasionally encouraged. Traditional African religions could be practised, cloaked in the forms of Christian worship. Parallels were soon drawn between the bondage of the Israelites and the bondage the slaves themselves experienced. These developments did not go unnoticed by the Jamaican Assembly:

> *The preaching and teaching of the sects called Baptist, Wesleyan Methodist and Moravians (but more especially the sect called Baptist) had the effect of producing in the minds of the slaves, a belief that they could not serve both a temporal and a spiritual master, thereby occasioning them to resist the lawful authority of their temporal, under the delusion of rendering themselves more acceptable to a spiritual master.*

The Jamaican Uprising of Christmas 1831, known also as Sam Sharpe's Revolt and the Baptist War, began in the west of the island, where the Baptists had a concentration of followers, and appears to have been triggered by the rumour that emancipation had already been granted. The plantation owners were suspected of keeping the fact of this decree from the slaves, so Sam Sharpe, a peripatetic Black Baptist deacon, reportedly encouraged his congregations to stop work on Christmas Day in order to achieve their goal.

Christmas 1831 fell on a Sunday. A mass downing of tools took place and, before Sharpe could impose order, open revolt fanned out across the island. As usual, militiamen were brought in to regain control of the affected plantations but they met with considerable resistance, as some of the slaves had already armed themselves and were banded together in a Black Regiment. It was a fortnight before order was fully restored, by which time over 200 Blacks and 14 Whites had been killed and property worth £1,132,440 been destroyed. In the aftermath 312 more rebels were executed.

BUSSA'S REBELLION

As work methods on the estates became more efficient, the role of slaves changed. Originally their tasks had been rudimentary, requiring them to be nothing more than unskilled agricultural labourers. But the economics of slavery required improvements in productivity. Many Africans had arrived in the Caribbean with skills in metallurgy and animal husbandry. Finally they would be given the opportunity to practise these skills. Later they were even brought into lower management, becoming overseers and drivers of labour gangs, and many worked as freelance artisans in the cities and towns.

Towards the end of slavery, therefore, the Black population was employed in a variety of lower-level management positions. There was now a diversified labour force with a broad range of skills, from craftsmen to warehouse clerks and port workers. In modern terms it was a management concept. Then the idea was simply and strategically to defuse the sense of subjection in an enslaved population. The ability of an African slave to move out of the field gang and become a driver, an overseer or even a manager of a household was seen as a major incentive.

An unforeseen by-product was a breakdown in the structure of discipline. Analysis of later slave rebellions shows that many were led by these newly promoted people – slaves who were regarded as privileged, as an elite, as living a life more free than their fellows. Bussa's Rebellion of 1816 is an example.

Bussa, now a national hero of Barbados, was the principal driver on his plantation. An African-born man, he was promoted up the system and became head manager of the labour force. His life would have been very comfortable, with all the privileges of lower management available to him, yet Bussa and other slaves like him organised a rebellion among the field slaves. Although only one Black man and one White man were killed, property was damaged on 12 plantations. A local militia of planters and settlers was swiftly drawn up to aid the British forces already stationed on the island.

The revolt was brutally put down and reprisals were swift and severe. A rear-admiral stationed in Barbados remarked: 'The militia, who could not be restrained by the same discipline as the troops, put many men, women and children to death, I fear without much discrimination.' One hundred and twenty slaves died either as a result of the fighting or upon capture and surrender. A further 144 were tried and executed. Luckiest of all were the 132 who found themselves deported.

A local government report into the rebellion said: 'We find it hard to believe that these very privileged peoples, these peoples in whom we had the greatest confidence and trust, whom we gave responsibilities and we gave material benefits, should be the ones to lead a rebellion against us.'

MAROONS

The most successful, long-running and, ultimately, ambivalent slave rebellion was a purely African affair, in no way connected with European attitudes to class, management or religion. The Maroons of Jamaica embodied several of the planters' worst nightmares. For over 80 years they had held out against the British in the mountains where they had established an isolated pocket of freedom for themselves. Since 1655 groups of runaway slaves had been fleeing plantations in western Jamaica and finding refuge in the surrounding hills. Dubbed 'Maroons', these runaways settled parts of the interior, farmed where they could and mounted raids on plantations on a regular basis. By the 1730s the Maroons were literally at war with the Redcoats. They had developed successful patterns of guerrilla warfare and they could rely on an active intelligence network among the plantation-bound slaves. For once the troops, militiamen, Indian guides and bloodhounds proved ineffective. By the 1730s the Maroon-held areas had effectively become the Jamaican Frontier. Fertile land lay within their territory and interested parties were pressuring the Jamaican Assembly to sue for peace in order to extend the plantation system into areas which would otherwise be vulnerable to attack.

In 1739 a treaty was drawn up between the Maroons and the British which gave the Maroons a declaration of peace and some land. There were two catches to this: firstly the Maroons had to agree not to take in any more runaway slaves; secondly, they had to assist the British authorities in capturing any runaways attempting to join them. The Maroons accepted these terms and the treaty was signed. So, in one stroke, the Jamaican Frontier had been pacified and the plantation system enlarged. It had even been provided with an auxiliary militia to call on should the need arise. The Maroons were as good as their word. Their actions thwarted the aspirations of many a fugitive for generations to come.

The ability to resist, and to develop a culture of resistance, varied from colony to colony and was influenced by the environment. In Jamaica and the Guyanas there were mountains and forests where a system of guerrilla warfare could be developed. Rebels could strike from remote strongholds and eventually vanish back into them. Colonies that provided that kind of cover usually produced independent Maroon societies.

In places where the environment did not support that kind of struggle, such as the Lesser Antilles, there was nowhere to retreat and a fight with imperial troops ran to its bitter end. This was the case in Barbados, where the Redcoats garrisoned in Bridgetown were able to suppress Bussa's Rebellion decisively and with ease.

THE PRESSURE ON THE SYSTEM

The role of slaves themselves in bringing down slavery was pivotal. In the last fifty years of slavery, as rebellions grew more sophisticated and more broad based, the colonial societies became unstable. After the Haitian Revolution in the 1790s slave owners in the British West Indies recognised, to their alarm, that slaves could overrun an entire island and seize control of its assets. Bussa's Rebellion and Sam Sharpe's Revolt show how slaves throughout the colonies were seeking to duplicate that experience.

By 1830, at the height of the emancipation debate in the British Parliament, it was clear that the only way slavery could be maintained in the West Indies was with military intervention. Since Parliament was not prepared to sanction that intervention, the only alternative was to reform the system.

Slave owners responded in a typically entrepreneurial way. They tried to appease the slave population – and protect their own interests – by toning down the harsher aspects of slavery. Slaves were granted certain rights: the right to marry, the right to have a family, the right to travel from plantation to plantation, the right to have festivals, the right to express themselves artistically, the right to be married in a Christian church and the right to become practising Anglicans. It was hoped these concessions would make slaves' lives more 'normal', and so reduce the hostility which the African people felt towards slave owners and slavery. But these belated acts of largesse were little more than the death throes of a passing culture. Change was in the air. For each concession granted the slaves demanded another, and in the end the one concession they all wanted was total emancipation.

BLACK RADICALS IN LONDON

By the last quarter of the 18th century London had become the largest Black metropolis outside the Americas. It was home to an estimated 10,000 to 15,000 people of African origin among its 800,000 residents. This community of servants, sailors, scribes, beggars and former slaves lent their voices to the clamour for abolition growing through the Black world at large. From the beginning of the anti-slavery agitation in Britain in the 1780s the testimonies of former slaves were crucial in exposing the harsh realities of the slave system and galvanising public opinion against it. A host of Black activists such as Robert Mandeville, Thomas Cooper, Jasper Goree and William Greene made their mark on Georgian and Regency London. 1787 saw the first major Black contribution to the campaign for abolition with the publication of Ottobah Cugoano's *Thoughts and sentiments on the evil and wicked traffic of the slavery and commerce of the human species.* For the first time British readers heard the authentic voice of slave witness. Cugoano, who had gained his freedom after being brought to London in his teens, insisted that slaves were morally obliged to rebel against their condition:

> *If any man should buy another man and compel him to*
> *his service and slavery without any agreement of that*
> *man to serve him, the enslaver is a robber and a*

defrauder of that man every day. Wherefore it is as much the duty of a man who is robbed in that manner to get out of the hands of his enslaver as it is for any honest community of men to get out of the hands of rogues and villains.

Driving home his argument, he pointed out that, as the British had gained 'a greater share in that iniquitous commerce than all the rest together', they should take the fastest steps towards emancipation.

Although Cugoano was the first published African critic of the slave trade, the most widely hailed Black activist was his friend Olaudah Equiano.

In 1788 *The Interesting Narrative of the Life of Olaudah Equiano, or Gustavus Vassa, the African* was published. It became a crucial text for the anti-slavery movement. The *General Magazine* commented:

> *The narrative appears to be written with much truth and simplicity . . . The reader, unless perchance he is a West India planter or Liverpool merchant, will find his humanity often severely wounded by the shameless barbarity practised towards the author's hapless countrymen in our colonies . . . That so unjust, so iniquitous a commerce may be abolished is our ardent wish.*

It was a best seller. Eight British editions of the *Narrative* appeared before Equiano's death, and six more followed in the next 22 years.

Equiano, an Igbo from Nigeria, had been captured by slavers at the age of 11. He arrived in Britain as a 12-year-old, having already experienced servitude in Barbados and Virginia. In London he was baptised and taught to read. He was later to serve all over the world in the British Navy, and even took part in an expedition to the Arctic in search of the North-west Passage from the Atlantic to the Pacific. During his travels he suffered the indignity of being re-sold to a Quaker merchant in Montserrat and, though he remained in bondage for three years, he managed to purchase his freedom and return to London.

Olaudah Equiano is often referred to as Britain's first Black political leader. He collaborated with Granville Sharp on a number of Black rights issues, most notably on the ill-fated Sierra Leone Scheme – a failed attempt to re-settle that part of West Africa with Black loyalists from Canada and Black beggars from London. Equiano, under the name 'Gustavus Vassa', was also a prolific journalist and correspondent. Reviewing a pro-planter pamphlet by Gordon Turnbull entitled *Apology for Negro Slavery: The West India planters vindicated from the Charge of Inhumanity*, he wrote:

> *To kidnap our fellow creatures, however they may differ in complexion, to degrade them into beasts of burden, to deny them every right but those, and scarcely those we allow to a horse, to keep them in perpetual servitude, is a crime as unjustifiable as it is cruel; but to avow and to defend this infamous traffic required the ability and the modesty of you and Mr. Tobin . . . Can any man be a Christian who asserts that one part of the human race were ordained to be in perpetual bondage to another?*

Equiano travelled the length and breadth of Britain promoting the cause of anti-slavery. In 1791 he toured Ireland for eight and a half months and sold nearly 2,000 copies of his book. Thomas Digges, a Belfast abolitionist, said Equiano was 'a principal instrument in bringing about the motion for a repeal of the Slave Act'.

A chorus of Black voices continued to carry the emancipatory refrain in the years after the abolition of the slave trade. Foremost of these was Robert Wedderburn, who was born in Jamaica in the 1760s and came to Britain in 1778. A chequered career saw him first as a sailor, then as a tailor, before he finally gained a licence to preach as a Unitarian minister in 1790. Safe in his new calling, he turned his wildly creative oratorical skills to pamphleteering. He started out with religious criticism. His first works laboured under titles such as *Truth, Self-supported; or, A refutation of certain doctrinal errors, generally adopted in the Christian Church* and *A shove for a heavy-breach'd Christian, crutches for the lame of faith, High-heeled shoes for dwarfs in holiness*. Wedderburn progressed to become the first disseminator of revolutionary anti-slavery material to the colonies. In 1824 he published *The Horrors of Slavery* and copies of his writings even came to the notice of the Jamaican Assembly. His work was unprecedented in its uncompromising stance. To the planters he said:

> *Prepare for flight, for the fate of St. Domingo (Haiti) awaits you. Get ready your blood hounds, the allies which you employed against the Maroons.*

And to his fellow Blacks:

You will need all of your strength to defend yourself
against those men who are now scheming in Europe
against the Blacks of St. Domingo.

His abiding motto was: 'It is degrading to human nature to petition your oppressors.'

Such exhortations found little favour with the authorities and Robert Wedderburn, preacher, propagandist and revolutionary, was fated to disappear into the black hole of the English penal system. He was last heard of in 1831 when, at the age of 68, he was sentenced to hard labour for affray. It is not known whether he survived long enough to receive news of the Emancipation Act two years later.

EMANCIPATION AND ITS AFTERMATH

Following a lull after the Abolition Act of 1807, the movement towards full emancipation was given new impetus in 1823 by the appearance of the Society for Mitigating and Gradually Abolishing the State of Slavery Throughout the British Dominions. This return to organised activity was the brainchild of William Wilberforce, Thomas Buxton and various Quakers. Their demands were not radical: slaves would be allowed to marry and own property; a slave's word would be accepted as evidence in court; Bible study was to be promoted; and working on Sundays would come to an end. Despite the lightweight nature of their programme, if not their title, the society's first annual report reveals the existence of 220 local branches and that 825 petitions had been presented to Parliament. In the following parliamentary session no fewer than 168,000 signatories – from London, Manchester, Glasgow and Edinburgh – would add their names to the 674 petitions aimed at slavery's abolition.

Seven years later the dormant Anti-Slavery Society was brought back to life. Its founding meeting was attended by 2,000 supporters, with 1,500 others turned away for lack of room. This society was headed yet again by Wilberforce and Buxton, who were taken by surprise by the overwhelming call for an immediate end to the slavery system. An 'agency committee' was created to build up the movement and soon there were 1,200 local societies. Hundreds of thousands of signatures found their way on to petitions.

Alongside this growth in organisation there was also a stream of fresh abolitionist literature. Henry Whiteley's *Three Months in Jamaica*, the most widely read anti-slavery pamphlet, linked the suffering of English working-class families with the oppression faced by slaves on the plantations. Within a month of publication 200,000 copies had been sold. As far as authentic slave literature was concerned, the most influential text of the 1830s was Mary Prince's *The History of Mary Prince, A West Indian Slave, Related by Herself*. Three editions appeared in its year of publication. Again the author associated conditions of labour in Britain with those found in the colonies. Her message was in tune with the current mood. Contrasting the experiences of the two sets of workers, she wrote:

> *If [the English] get a bad master, they give warning and go hire to another. They have their liberty. That's what we want. We don't mind hard work, if we had proper treatment and proper wages like English servants, and proper time given in the week to keep us from breaking the Sabbath. But they won't give it; they will have work – work – work, night and day, sick and*

*well, till we are quite done up; and we must not speak
up nor look amiss, however much we be abused. And
then, when we are quite done up, who cares for us
more than for a lame horse? This is slavery. I tell it to
let English people know the truth; and I hope they will
never leave off to pray to God, and call loud to the
great King of England, till all the poor blacks be given
free, and slavery done up for evermore.*

All this activity was taking place in 1831 against the background
of Sam Sharpe's Revolt in Jamaica. This was a potentially
disastrous time for the abolitionists as the planters and their
spokesmen in Parliament seized upon that incident to besmirch
the anti-slavery cause, conflating the growth of liberal thought
with the prospect of Black unruliness. The ploy failed thanks to
the testimonies of the Nonconformist preachers who had been
beaten, tarred, feathered and deported from Jamaica on
suspicion of being involved with the revolt. Public attention was
now focused on the brutality of the repression and the
callousness of its apologists in Parliament. The final corner was
being turned. The British slave system was on its last legs and
emancipation only a few years away.

The Abolition of Slavery Act, passed in August 1833, was
scheduled to come into force in August the following year. Its
success was not entirely due to slave rebellions, grass-roots
petitioning and the logistics of military control. As usual, the
lures of money and continued profit were brought to bear.

From the beginnings of the abolition movement its
parliamentary supporters had been reassuring planters that
emancipation would not affect their labour supply. The promise

was held out that the emancipated Blacks would remain under some coercion. Vagrancy laws were proposed under which slaves attempting to leave the plantations would be penalised and land-ownership beyond the range of garden plots would be illegal. There was also to be a period of 'apprenticeship' (in the act's final draft a six-year term was agreed upon) during which planters had the right to the continuing labour of their 'ex-slaves'. As Thomas Buxton put it:

> It may be extremely necessary for the state to introduce laws for protecting persons from living in idleness to the detriment of the state.

Such views, of course, were approved at the Colonial Office, where the assumptions underlying this position were stated more forcefully:

> A state of things where the negro escaped the necessity for labour would be as bad for him as for his owner. He would be cut off from civilising influences, would have no incentive to better his condition or to impose any but the slightest degree of discipline on himself. Thus he might well become a more degraded being than his ancestors in Africa.

This appeasement of the planters' racism was made all the more seductive by the promise of inordinate financial compensation. A government which in 1834 was proving reluctant to furnish additional funds towards poor relief in England somehow found the means to guarantee the West Indian planters between £15 million and £20 million worth of compensation. With the spectre of revolt still hovering, the slave owners took the bait. Rather than run the risk of further conflict that might destroy their property they looked with favour on parliamentary legislation that would not only free the slaves but offer substantial compensation.

Seen in this light, the emancipation law was a moderate measure, in that it compensated not the slaves, who had built up the wealth of Britain through centuries of unpaid labour, but the former slave owners.

This fundamental injustice was not to be forgotten by the former slaves or their descendants. This is how our contemporary Robert Beckford reacted when faced with the plantation records he came across in Jamaica:

> *The account is incredibly cold and highly detailed and it shows that they were dealing with pieces of property. The slaves are not represented as human beings; they are property, economic units. And the government obviously was very keen to see that the slave owners were compensated, and although this meant that slaves would go free, the main focus is that slave owners are compensated for their lack of property – and that's what they are in this book. My ancestors here are property, economic units.*
>
> *The parliamentary records show that William Beckford was compensated for the loss of his slaves after the abolition of slavery. From my calculations roughly £20,000 was paid in compensation to William Beckford and members of his family just for the slaves in Jamaica. The slaves received absolutely nothing. And they had to eke out a living after slavery. The*

record shows that many of them earned a shilling a day for cutting cane. And I know from my own family history that my grandfather on my mother's side was still making a shilling a day in 1935, so it took a long time for the descendants of the slaves to move out of that kind of oppressive economic system.

With the exception of a few Nonconformist church festivals, Emancipation Day, 1 August 1834, went largely uncelebrated and unnoticed in Jamaica and Britain's other West Indian colonies. The Black population had other concerns. A fresh raft of law-and-order measures had been introduced. Under their new conditions of 'apprenticeship', slaves were still obliged to stay on the plantations and put in a ten-hour day. Absenteeism would result in imprisonment in one of the many new jails (equipped with treadmills) which were being built to contain recalcitrant workers. Additional tiers of 'special officers' and stipendiary magistrates were created to police the changes. 'Apprentices', females included, could still be flogged without redress. The apprenticeship scheme would come to an end only in 1838 after the Anti-Slavery Society, following an inspection tour of the West Indian colonies in 1836, had produced another barrage of petitions and pamphlets.

Apart from an overall decline in the plantation economy, the effects of emancipation in the British West Indies varied from island to island. Yearly sugar production slumped by 36% between 1824-33 and 1839-46. As output dropped, the price of sugar rose and 50% of the Jamaican plantations went out of business. In Trinidad and British Guyana the newly freed slaves initiated a series of large-scale strikes over a 30-year period which obliged local planters to import 96,580 indentured labourers from the Indian sub-continent. Barbados and Antigua, with their large resident White populations, managed not only to maintain but to increase their rates of production, while Black and Coloured people remained disenfranchised due to property-owning qualifications. In Jamaica the workers were offered a daily wage (originally six to eight pence, later increased to one shilling) but were also required to pay rent.

The most positive result of emancipation was the growth of a class of independent Black craftspeople and traders. By 1844 there were 2,500 in Antigua, 6,000 in British Guyana, 12,000 in Barbados and 17,500 in Jamaica. All West Indian colonies experienced increases in Black private ownership of property and in school attendance by Black children. Despite these changes, by the late 1860s sugar production in the colonies had again risen to pre-emancipation levels.

The lavish compensation paid out to the slave owners failed to find its way back into the developing economy of the West Indies. Rather than using these funds to facilitate an effective transition from slavery to free labour, the planters invested them in the English bond market and acquired property in England.

Perhaps the most ironic outcome of the whole abolitionist enterprise was the way in which it was hijacked by the British establishment. Having cleansed itself of the taint of slavery, the British government sought to re-brand itself in the guise of a roving anti-slavery watchdog. But the mission to suppress slavery on a global scale also served as a means of checking the naval ambitions of other European powers.

The policing of slavery on the west coast of Africa coincided with a heightening of European interest in the African interior. The main instrument in this new policy was the British West Africa Squadron. This force of six ships was supposed to patrol the African coast from Angola to the Cape Verde Islands, blockade ports, seize slaving ships and protect legitimate British traders. The squadron, however, was in no condition to do this. Lord Palmerston once described how, 'if there was a particularly old, slow-going tub in the navy, she was sure to be sent to the coast of Africa to try and catch the fast-sailing American clippers'. In practice, the only area that could be effectively policed was Benin and Sierra Leone. There were other problems: only vessels actually carrying slaves could be stopped; and a ship entering a port with the express intention of slaving was beyond the law. This led to farcical scenes such as that related by Captain Joseph Denman:

> We had no power over the ship till the slaves were on board. The consequence was that if a man-of-war lay in a port full of slavers, as I have seen in Whydah, with ten or a dozen . . . at one time, as long as the man-of-war was in port they would not ship their slaves; directly the man-of-war was out of sight, they shipped their slaves, and every vessel in the harbour would weigh their anchor and set sail. The cruiser would probably chase the wrong ship and, after 100 miles, would be laughed at by the master of that vessel, who would say that he had only put on sail for a pasatiempo.

Even when slaves were released, as 35,000 were in the 1830s, the majority ended up being sent to labour in Freetown, while the rest consented to travel on to British colonies as 'apprentices'.

The only British national tried for trading in slaves was Pedro Zulueta, a naturalised Briton of Spanish origin. He was a commercial agent and banker to Pedro Blanco, the leading slave trader in West Africa in the 1840s, and was brought to trial in 1843, charged with direct involvement in the slave trade there. His case was unusual, firstly in being tried at all but also because the prosecution was brought against him privately, though the papers had originally been brought before the government and he had testified before a select committee of Parliament in 1842. After one-and-a-half hours' deliberation the jury found him not guilty – a decision greeted with jubilation in the court and in much of the press. The central argument in support of Zulueta was that he was a British manufacturer doing what any good British manufacturer should do – supplying his clients with merchandise (in this instance ships).

In 1839 the Society for the Extinction of the Slave Trade and the Civilisation of Africa was founded by Sir Thomas Buxton. Presiding over it was Queen Victoria's consort, Prince Albert. Eighteen bishops, 15 earls, eight marquises, five dukes and four archbishops were among its vice-presidents. After almost 60 years the cause of abolition finally acquired the royal seal of approval.

Some aspects of abolitionism dovetailed neatly with expansionist policies and patriotic sentiment. Buxton was keen to see the regeneration of Africa primarily through a series of trading posts along the river Niger. His ideas, encapsulated in his 1838 book *The African Slave Trade and Its Remedy*, quickly gained acceptance among members of the establishment, who foresaw the coming of an Africa colonised and controlled by Europeans, though without slavery.

Britain was determined to be in the forefront of European expansion in Africa. Having established its anti-slavery patrol along the west coast, it exercised an influence in the area which inevitably aided British business. Trading links grew steadily through the 19th century. The export of cotton goods from Britain to West Africa had increased thirtyfold between the beginning of the century and the 1830s. At the same time it encouraged 'legitimate' trade, with West Africa in particular, especially in connection with the lucrative (and slave-based) trade in palm oil.

In the wake of abolition Britain intervened more and more directly in Africa. It established its first colonies in West Africa – in Sierra Leone and then Lagos. It was the beginning of what became, by the end of the century, the 'Scramble for Africa' – the struggle among European powers to colonize and dominate the continent. The British carried their new morality with the goods they traded. The abolitionist campaign was taken into the interior of West Africa and gunboat diplomacy was used to encourage African rulers to abolish the slave trade in their own dominions. The campaign met with some resistance. As early as 1807 the King of Bonny had expressed his fears in a letter to the Liverpool trader, Captain Hugh Crow: 'We think that this trade must go on. That is the verdict of our oracle and the priests. They say that your country, however great, can never stop a trade ordained by God himself.' Things changed slowly.

Meanwhile the slave trade was still flourishing in other parts of the world, most notably in Brazil and Cuba. Although forbidden under British law, the British still found ways to profit from the trade. The merchants and bankers of London and Liverpool turned their attention to the remaining markets. Slaving voyages were still directly financed by the City of London, and slave ships custom-built in the dockyards of Bristol and Liverpool. Such activity, naturally, was supported by the still powerful planters' lobby in Parliament, as Dr Hakim Adi explains:

> *There was a West Indian lobby in the sense that there were still West Indian commercial interests which had their representatives in Parliament, but perhaps more importantly there were other commercial and industrial interests that also had their representatives in Parliament, and in other parts of government. And so they were a very powerful lobbying group to make sure that nothing was done to stop what was essentially Britain's trade with other parts of the world. They would have argued, for example, that British manufacturers couldn't be held responsible for what happened to the goods which they produced. They didn't know where they were going to end up or what they were going to be exchanged for. What was important was that they produced, they exported and profits were realised. These were the kind of arguments that were continually raised, and which prevented laws being enforced which might have stopped this trade. And indeed, for the rulers of Britain, there was no reason to stop this kind of commercial activity. That was what Britain was about in the middle of the nineteenth century.*

Nevertheless the patriotic view prevailed that the British were leading the world in a moral crusade. In 1850 the Prime Minister, Lord Russell, felt free to crow:

> *It appears to me that if we give up this high and holy work, and proclaim ourselves to be no longer fitted to lead in the championship against the curse and the crime of slavery, we have no longer a right to expect a continuance of those blessings, which by God's favour, we have enjoyed. I think the high, the moral and the Christian character of this nation is the main source and secret of its strength.*

In reality the main source and secret of the nation's strength, both before and long after slavery, was the ingenuity which allowed commerce to thrive under altered circumstances, and which could transform the noble cause of abolition into a tool for imperial expansion into the heart of Africa.

PART FOUR

THE LEGACY

THE POLITICAL
LEGACY

The anti-slavery movement was the first genuine mass movement this country had seen. It held appeal for almost all classes and sectors of British society. From labourers to lords, from domestics to duchesses, support for the abolitionist position reached a level unprecedented in Britain's history. 'Never,' wrote Samuel Whitbread, 'had the country expressed so general a feeling as they had about the slave trade; if they had, Parliament would long since have been reformed.'

A parallel may be drawn with the current international trade in arms. After the United States, Britain is probably the biggest arms trader in the world. No one denies the human cost of this commerce – that it results in the deaths of tens of thousands of comparatively innocent men, women and children. But, despite our well-recorded distaste, the arms trade continues to flourish. It is seen as an economic necessity. This, more or less, was the same perspective that people had on slavery until the second half of the 18th century. People said: it has always been there, it is vital for the economy and, if we do not do it, other countries will.

The political legacies of such a large-scale change of direction remain. The abolitionist movement employed new methods of mass-communication in an attempt to reach potential supporters. The anti-slavers' emblem and motto – a chained Black man on one knee asking the onlooker: 'Am I not a man and a brother?' – became a common sight. This device, designed and marketed by Josiah Wedgwood, appeared on tableware, jewellery, pamphlets and posters all over the country. Brooches and pendants proclaiming adherence to abolitionist ideals proved essential in garnering support from sectors of society normally beyond the reach of political ideas.

Even more fundamental to the growth of the movement was the proliferation of petitions that abolitionism engendered. Until the late 1780s petitioning for a redress of grievance had posed little threat to parliamentary authority. The overwhelming majority of petitions had been of a purely commercial nature. The anti-slavery movement changed that forever. Petitions became a political weapon. The day of the middle-class petition was over and working-class radicalism was taking a huge leap forward.

Signatories to these new waves of anti-slavery petitions were predominantly from working-class backgrounds. The numbers speak for themselves. In 1788 more than 100 petitions appeared in support of the cause. Manchester alone furnished 10,639 signatures. In 1792 519 petitions were submitted in support of Wilberforce's proposed abolition bill. On this occasion the number of signatures from Manchester (then with a population of 75,000) was 20,000.

British radical leaders were quick to link these new developments with the growing demand for domestic reform. Thomas Hardy, founder of the London Corresponding Society, spoke publicly of how liberty for Blacks and liberty for Whites were indivisible. Major John Cartwright, dubbed by some 'The Father of Reform', wrote:

> *Should the West Indian slaves, who but the other day had not the slightest prospect of such an event, find themselves emancipated, who can say that there is no hope of our constitutional rights and liberties being restored?*

In 1814, within a single month, 1,500,000 signatures found their way on to over 800 anti-slavery petitions; and between 1826 and 1832 the House of Lords alone received more than 3,500 petitions.

The use of petitions proved radical in more ways than had originally been intended. The reformist sentiments of the petitioners had yet to extend to women. Only adult male signatures were accepted as valid and the foremost opponent of female participation in the abolition process was none other than William Wilberforce. In response to the unexpected degree of female involvement in the movement, he wrote:

> *All private exertions for such an object become their character, but for ladies to meet, to go from house to house stirring up petitions – these appear to me proceedings unsuited to the female character as delineated in scripture.*

Wilberforce, like most male activists, was little prepared for the torrent of political activity women would produce independently on behalf of his movement.

A great spur to this activity came in the writings of middle- and upper-class women such as Hannah More and Lady Middleton, who proved to be some of anti-slavery's most effective advocates and pamphleteers. The women's resolve, in many instances, was greater than that of the men. In response to the formation in 1823 of the Society for Mitigating and Gradually Abolishing the State of Slavery Throughout the British Dominions, a pamphlet (first published anonymously) entitled *Immediate Not Gradual Emancipation* appeared in 1824. Its author, Mrs Elizabeth Heyricke, outlined a number of positions, most of them uncompromising, which exemplified the difference in perspective between male and female activists.

> *Away then with the puerile cant about gradual emancipation. Let the galling ignominious chains of slavery be struck off, at once, from these abused and suffering, these patient, magnanimous creatures . . .*
> *The restoration of the poor Negroes' liberty must be the beginning of our colonial reform, the first act of justice, the pledge of our sincerity. It is the only solid foundation on which the reformation of the slave, and the still more needful reformation of his usurping master, can be built.*

Concessionary measures, by which a number of women's groups were allowed to affiliate themselves to local abolitionist societies, gave greater voice to such feelings and the chairwoman of one group was heard to declare: 'men may propose only *gradually* to abolish the worst of crimes, and only to *mitigate* the most evil bondage . . . I trust no ladies' association will ever be found with such words attached to it.'

The Sheffield Female Anti-Slavery Society made the following appeal from the 'Friends of the Negro' to the British people in 1827:

> *Slavery is not exclusively a political but pre-eminently a moral question; one, therefore, on which the humble-minded reader of the Bible, which enriches his cottage shelf is, immeasurably, a better politician than the statesman versed in the intrigues of Cabinets. We ought to obey God rather than man.*

By 1831 there were over 40 established ladies' anti-slavery groups and their agenda (as expressed, for instance, in the charming title of the Birmingham Ladies Negro's Friend Society) was staunch in its demand for emancipation. Largely unsupported by their male counterparts, women were eventually left alone to compile their own petitions. In 1833 the Glasgow Ladies Anti-Slavery Society could summon up to 1,800 women to its meetings. It drew up a petition which was signed by 350,000 women. For hundreds of thousands of women throughout Britain participation in the abolitionist struggle would mark their first entry into politics.

In 1840 the artist Benjamin Robert Haydon set about painting a group portrait of the delegates to that year's Anti-Slavery Convention. On hearing of the exclusion of female campaigners from the picture, Anne Knight wrote to the activist Lucy Townsend, declaring:

I am very anxious that the historical picture now in the hand of Haydon should not be performed without the chief lady of the history being there in justice to history and posterity the person who established women's anti-slavery groups. You have as much right to be there as Thomas Clarkson himself, nay perhaps more. His achievement was in the slave trade; thine was slavery itself in the pervading movement.

Unwittingly, anti-slavery had provided a springboard for the nascent women's consciousness movement. The coalitions of female activists brought about by involvement here would later figure prominently in the push for women's suffrage.

Abolitionism also produced another long-lasting result. For most White Britons, working class and otherwise, anti-slavery was their first introduction to any form of Black consciousness. By assimilating slave narratives such as those produced by Equiano, Cugoano and Mary Prince into their own struggles for representation and reform future generations of radicals, in Britain and beyond, were able to use aspects of Black activism to underpin their own agendas and working-class organisations expressed their demands in similar terms.

Outside the political arena, however, everyday relationships between Blacks and Whites, particularly on the streets of Britain's major cities, would prove more problematic.

THE CULTURAL
LEGACY

In 1840 J.M.W. Turner's painting *The Slave Ship* was first exhibited at the Royal Academy. Its full title was *Slavers throwing overboard the dead and dying – Typhoon coming on*. The painting portrays a stormy sea scene. The waves in the foreground are russet-coloured, gold and white. At the base of the picture the viewer can discern a mess of manacled black limbs splashing in the bloody water. The drowning figures are surrounded by diverse fish and seafowl. From the right-hand corner an unclassifiable leviathan surges forward to partake of the feast. In the background, half hidden amid swathes of baleful yellow light, a slaving ship with sails furled is drifting away from the massacre.

Though the picture is often seen as representing the climax of the artist's middle period, its full cultural implications are usually overlooked. *The Slave Ship* represents an incident that was central to the growth of the abolition movement: the case of the slaver *Zong*.

The *Zong* was bound for Jamaica in November 1781 with a crew of 17 and a cargo of 470 slaves. In mid-Atlantic the ship was struck by an epidemic. The master, Captain Luke Collingwood, had an insurance policy which guaranteed reimbursement for slaves lost at sea but offered no compensation for those dead on arrival. Working on the assumption that a number of his cargo would perish anyway, he dumped 133 live slaves into the sea, many of them still in shackles.

The ship's first mate, initially opposed to his captain's plans, was informed that 'it would not be so cruel to throw the poor sick wretches into the sea as to suffer them to linger out a few days under the disorders with which they were afflicted'.

Collingwood was brought to trial back in England. The charge was murder. Despite a vigorous campaign launched by Granville Sharp, Olaudah Equiano and other abolitionists, Collingwood and his crew walked free and went on to claim £3,960 compensation against the loss of their 'chattels and goods'.

In common with much of Turner's subject matter (from *The Burning of the Houses of Parliament* to *Rain, Steam and Speed – the Great Western Railway*) *The Slave Ship* demonstrated his skill at choosing a topic of wide appeal. By 1838 Parliament had officially signalled the end of Britain's involvement in the slave trade. By rendering the *Zong* incident in oils, Turner not only condemns the past atrocity but applauds Britain's withdrawal from slavery. The artist has captured the mood of his times. Abolitionism, as far as the British are concerned, has triumphed and they have taken the leading part in it. So Turner is painting a memory of horrors whilst saluting the contemporary sense of moral victory.

In order to appreciate the cultural significance of Turner's picture, we must look at the wider context of arts in Britain, and their response to the issues of slavery.

Abolition was the first major philanthropic movement in this country. It coincided with new ideas coming from France about liberty and fraternity, as well as ideas about the rights of man and the freedom of the individual in the face of political and social tyrannies. It was natural that the movement was supported by poets and artists, coinciding as it did with the Romantic movement which was itself built on the notions of freedom of spirit and individual truth. To adopt an anti-slavery position was to be part of the spirit of the age.

In some of William Blake's prints we are shown the enormous suffering of slaves who rebelled and the torture visited upon their bodies. Blake presents them in grotesque postures of pain to shock people into realising what slavery was really about. It was about torturing people and stripping them not just of dignity but literally of their flesh.

The universities also played a role in this. Cambridge became a hive of intellectual activity on behalf of abolition. Peter Peckard, the vice-chancellor, was a leading abolitionist and Clarkson and Wilberforce were associated with the university. Intellectuals and artists were galvanised by the idea of the African as an icon of all human suffering, especially that of the poor.

Although the 'noble savage' was to become a standard feature of 18th-century literature, the suffering Black figure was not an original idea. In 1657 there was the tragic tale of Yarico, a native Barbadian woman, whose misfortune was to save the life of the very Christian who would impregnate her prior to the inevitable betrayal. This legend appeared in 40 incarnations (plays, poems, ballet and opera) and eight languages. Aphra

Behn's novel *Oroonooko* followed in 1678. Thomas Southerne's dramatisation of this featured almost yearly on the London stage for the next hundred years and prepared the way for a reworking of the fettered Negro motif in the works of Blake, Robert Burns, William Cowper and others. Yet unlike American literature, which produced Harriet Beecher Stowe's *Uncle Tom's Cabin* among other works, English letters produced little memorable on the subject of slavery.

One of the few books in which anti-slavery ideas did appear was Daniel Defoe's *History of the Pyrates*. Published in 1724, it tells of a French buccaneer, Captain Misson, whose belief that 'every man was born free and had as much right to what would support him as the air he respired' led him to found the colony of Libertalia, where slavery was outlawed and slaves released from captivity in other colonies were welcome to settle. But Defoe's more successful works, such as *Robinson Crusoe* and *Colonel Jack*, were little more than colonial romances in which the 'noble savage' found comfort in voluntary servitude.

One of the earliest writers to make the link between the suffering of slaves in the colonies and workers in Britain was Oliver Goldsmith. His poem 'The Traveller' first appeared in 1763:

> *When I behold a factious band agree*
> *To call it freedom when themselves are free;*
> *Each wanton judge new penal statutes draw,*
> *Laws grind the poor, and rich men rule the law;*
> *The wealth of climes, where savage nations roam,*
> *Pillag'd from slaves to purchase slaves at home;*
> *Fear, pity, justice, indignation start,*
> *Tear off reserve, and bare my swelling heart . . .*

Wordsworth's sonnet dedicated to Toussaint L'Ouverture and published in 1803 is the best poetic expression of the growing pro-abolition climate:

> *Though fallen thyself, never to rise again,*
> *Live, and take comfort. Thou hast left behind*
> *Powers that will work for thee; air, earth, and skies;*
> *There's not a breathing of the common wind*
> *That will forget thee; thou hast great allies;*
> *Thy friends are exultations, agonies,*
> *And love, and man's unconquerable mind.*

Yet even William Wordsworth was to fall in line with prevailing sentiment as a poem about the little Black boy 'whose soul was white' attests.

James Thomson's widely read poem 'The Seasons' (1726-30) is almost alone in dealing directly with the subject of human traffic. Here he describes a shark's attraction to a slave-ship:

> *Lured by the scent*
> *Of steaming crowds, of rank disease and death,*
> *Behold! He rushing, cuts the briny flood,*
> *Swift as the gale can bear the ship along;*
> *And from the partners of that cruel trade,*
> *Which spoils unhappy Guinea of her sons,*
> *Demands his share of prey – demands themselves!*

With the literary legacy largely composed of more understated affectations of gentlemanly outrage, modern readers tend to feel a continual sense of something missing. The prevailing attitude is summed up in William Cowper's ironic poem of 1788, 'Pity for Poor Africans':

> *I own I am shocked by the purchase of slaves,*
> *And fear those who buy them and sell them are knaves;*
> *What I hear of their hardships, their tortures and groans,*
> *Is almost enough to drive pity from stones.*
>
> *I pity them greatly, but I must be mum,*
> *For how could we do without sugar and rum?*

The majority of 18th- and 19th-century writing, however, is remarkable for dancing round realities of plantation life. The author Mike Phillips has pointed out numerous examples of this type of avoidance.

In *Mansfield Park*, for instance, Mr Bertram, the wealthy entrepreneur, is suddenly called away on business to Barbados. Nowhere does Jane Austen detail the origins of Bertram's wealth or the nature of his 'business'. In her unfinished novel *Sanditon*, she introduces the wealthy 'mulatto' heiress, Miss Lambe, whom Lady Denham encourages her son, Sir Edward, to pursue.

In Thackeray's *Vanity Fair* an another English family (Mr Osborne and his daughters) is eager to see a 'mulatto' heiress (the crudely-named Miss Swartz) marry into it. Miss Swartz is interesting inasmuch as the characteristics she displays – vulgarity, good-naturedness and simple-mindedness – are in tune with the qualities attributed to Black people at that time. In response to the family's entreaties, the younger Osborne retorts: 'Marry that mulatto woman? I don't like her colour, sir. Ask the black that sweeps opposite Fleet Street, sir. I'm not going to marry a Hottentot Venus.'

The novels of the Brontës contain dark hints of one repercussion of the slave trade that is never faced directly. In *Jane Eyre* there is the peculiar figure of the first Mrs Rochester, the 'Creole' whose 'bad blood', it is implied, lies at the root of her insanity. Most tellingly, there is Heathcliff in *Wuthering Heights*, a swarthy skinned Liverpudlian foundling of possible 'Lascar origin'.

The author and critic Professor Gretchen Gerzina sees in these novels the first literary expressions of the fears that the Black presence holds for British society:

> *One thing that happens with the Victorians in literature is because you don't have that constant relentless visual presence of Black people in Britain at the time, they begin to make their way into the fiction in very oblique and obscure ways. They become the mysterious stranger from abroad who has a secret, perhaps a genetic secret, so you get a novel like* Jane Eyre *in which she is trying to become the real wife of Rochester, and you find that he's got a wife who's locked away in the attic and she's got a problem. You begin to realise, as you read back, that she has most likely got a racial identity that he finds insupportable. So you've got a woman in the attic who has come from the West Indies, who's got a family secret that has to do with her background and her history and her health, and she has to be burned up at the end of the book in order for Jane to become the real wife.*
>
> *So you begin to see in the Victorian period a lot of fear of Black people – who have a slave back-ground – infiltrating their way into the Victorian*

world, and it's a great terror to many people to think it's not out there somewhere, it's back here in the house, it's in your wife, it's in your attic. And people like the Brontës were able to use that, I think, in ways that critics now are only beginning to think about . . .

I think you begin to see in the mid-nineteenth century a really surprising phenomenon, which is that race and slavery had been a very clear-cut issue. You might be conflicted about how you felt about it, but it didn't affect you personally in any real way. If you didn't own a slave or you didn't own a plantation in the West Indies you weren't necessarily affected by it. Once that issue goes away [after abolition] and you're not sure what's happened to the people, you begin to get this psychological phenomenon, a kind of fear of not being quite sure who you might be or who your neighbours might be. And it becomes something that snakes into the brain in a way that is much less overt and much less comfortable to deal with.

These fictional portrayals of Black people offer a host of insights into the state of the post-abolition British psyche. Gerzina again:

If you can say, on the one hand, that we've gotten rid of slavery and it no longer exists, we can now use it as a weapon against the Americans who beat us in the War of Independence and are now involved in another one [the American Civil War].

At the same time, slavery is no longer a heated political issue and it's open to all sorts of interpretations. You can make fun of people in ways that you couldn't before if you were affecting people's livelihoods . . . The abolition of the slave trade freed White Britons in a way that you hadn't seen before. Perhaps not as greatly as you might be led to believe, but it freed them to say this is no longer a hot potato. We can now play with this issue, we can either bring it into our books if we think it's important and people want to read about it, we can make fun of those who still think it's an issue, or we can rely on it to die quietly and then bring it back in new ways as it becomes profitable in fiction.

What I think it says about the British people is that they're very willing to embrace an idea, an issue, a kind of theme song. But then if it's not interesting and it's not the issue of the day, it goes away, it's fashionable to ignore it . . . So I think it says that although the British were very open to ideas about race that were exaggerations, they were very unprepared to deal with the idea of race as it might exist in their own midst. They were able to take the idea of slavery and turn it, in some cases, into Gothic fiction, which is why you see Black people depicted in . . . a lot of Gothic novels where you have ghosts, you have goblins, you have fears – and that fear gets really internalised.

The purely decorative arts had an active part to play in the campaign against slavery. From the 1780s Britain was flooded with abolition images, many of which were produced by the Wedgwood factory. These came in the form of plates, earrings, signet rings, statues and any other kind of artefact upon which abolition principles could be inscribed. The most common image was of a kneeling Black man with hands enchained asking, 'Am I not a man and a brother?' It was a question hard to answer in the negative.

The impact of an appeal to Christian sentiment should not be underestimated. According to Professor David Dabydeen:

> *Practically everybody in the eighteenth century was a Christian. Church-going was still something that you did seriously. So therefore when the story of the good Samaritan was read to you from the pulpit and you came out of the church and saw a Black beggar, maybe begging outside the church, or you came across an abolitionist print, then you would automatically, in a sense almost unconsciously, connect the story of the good Samaritan to the story of the African.*

Through popular art, ordinary people came into constant contact with images of Black suffering and with calls for justice and humanity, all of which, by increasing awareness, helped to stimulate and strengthen the anti-slavery movement.

The pro-slavery lobby had its own, very different imagery. Unable to take the moral high ground or make use of any appreciable artistic licence, its supporters invoked pseudo-science. The effects on popular perceptions resonate to this day.

The history of 'scientific' justifications for the slave trade is long and bizarre. Long before any contact was established between English and African peoples, the concept of blackness held negative connotations. Some were inherent, as in the memory of the Black Death; others were metaphorical, as in references to black magic, the black arts, blackmail, black sheep, blacklists, blackguards and all other types of baseness including the complexion of the devil himself. In the fourth century St Jerome wrote: 'Born of the Devil, we are black.' In the eleventh century Satan, as a 'blackamoore', visited St Margaret, Queen of Scotland. In 1603 the future Archbishop of York, Samuel Harsnet, wrote of a woman to whom the evil one had appeared in the form of 'a black man standing at the door and beckoning her to come away'.

Rather than provoking a re-assessment and recon-figuration of these concepts, the English encounter with Africa was allowed to reaffirm them and make them concrete. Blackness of skin was taken to be synonymous with diabolical intentions. It was on sound precedent then that Sir Thomas Herbert, an English traveller in Africa in the 1620s, could report that the inhabitants were 'devilish savages' and 'devils incarnate', some of whom worshipped Beelzebub in 'the form of a bloody dragon'.

It was a short step from demonology to bestiality, given what the historian Peter Fryer refers to as the perceived 'similarity between the human-like beasts of the "Dark continent" and that continent's supposedly beast-like human beings'. Tales abounded of human-simian copulation, sexual degeneracy and cannibalism. This account comes from Sir Thomas Herbert:

> *Not satisfied with nature's treasures . . . the de-*
> *struction of men and women neighbouring them,*
> *whose dead carcasses they devour with a vulture's*
> *appetite; whom if they miss, they serve their friends (so*
> *they mis-call them) such scurvy sauce, butchering*
> *them, thinking they excuse all in a complement, that*

they know no rarer way to express true love than in making (not two souls) two bodies in an inseparable union: yea, some (worne by age, or worme-eaten by the pox) proffer themselves to the shambles, and accordingly are jointed and set to upon the stalls.

Building on this body of disinformation, 18th-century writers such as the Scottish judge Lord Monboddo could confidently inform his readers that orang-utans were human beings incapable of speech and a 'barbarous nation' which 'carried off boys and girls as slaves and kept them for years without harming them'. They also buried their dead and 'played very well on pipes, harps and other instruments'.

Before long numerous armchair demagogues, such as Edward Long, a Jamaican planter, were peddling fanciful stuff. His 23-volume *Universal History*, in 1736, has these reflections on Africans, presumably gleaned from those he worked to death on his own plantations:

[Africans are] proud lazy, treacherous, thievish, hot and addicted to all kinds of lusts, and most ready to promote them in others, as pimps, panders, incestuous, brutish and savage, cruel and revengeful, devourers of human flesh, and quaffers of human blood, inconstant, base, treacherous and cowardly; fond of and addicted to all sorts of superstition and witchcraft; and in a word to every vice that came their way, or within their reach . . . It is hardly possible to find in any African any quality but what is of the bad kind: they are inhumans, drunkards, deceitful, extremely covetous, and perfidious to the highest degree. We need not add

to these their impurities and blasphemies, because in these they outdo all other nations, Africa being known to have been ever burning with innumerable impurities; insomuch that one would rather take it for a volcano of the most impure flames, than for a habitation of human creatures . . .

Thus much shall suffice for the general character of the native Africans . . . it is so far from being either unjust or exaggerated, with regard to the far greater part of them, that in many instances they deserve, if possible, a much more odious one; they being in many parts so utterly void of all humanity, and even natural affection, that parents will sell their wives and children, and vice versa, for slaves into the American colonies, even for so small a matter as a gallon or two of brandy.

The pro-slavery lobby was not slow in putting these myths to good use. According to Professor David Dabydeen:

Whenever there was a slavery vote, support for abolition inevitably dipped in the country because the propagandists would talk about Black people ravishing White womanhood, eating babies, howling through the plantation house smashing down the china, tearing up the books – in other words, presenting them as wild and ferocious animals who needed to be tamed, trained and restrained. So you had two sets of competing imagery in the art as well as in the literature of the period.

From such beginnings sprang the entire school of 'scientific racism'. Its arch exponent Edward Long, starting from the assumption that heredity was a greater influence on human character than environment, theorised that Black people belonged to a different species. In his *Candid Reflections*, published in 1772, he warned that 'hybrids' between the Black and White races would eventually be infertile and that Black people were closer to apes than human beings. In the following century, Charles Darwin, while maintaining that humanity shared a common African origin, also subscribed to the idea of a 'great chain of Being', at the bottom of which were Black and Irish people. Needless to say the Anglo-Saxon variety of humanity was at the summit. The effects of such notions are still with us. The geneticist Dr Steve Jones explains:

> *'Scientific racism' is a pair of words which all geneticists or biologists have been told to fear and hate, there's no question of that. There's a good reason why that should be so and I suppose most people are aware of it. It was used as an alibi for some of the great crimes of the nineteenth and the twentieth centuries.*
>
> *Having said that, there is no reason why there shouldn't be a science of race. We are animals, after all; we can study genes over the world. We know more about our own genes than any other species'. The interesting thing is that there's always been a fear of the other. As people began to move from Europe, first into North Africa and India, then to all the rest of the world, there was an automatic response to see these people as less than human. To identify somebody as different was almost automatically to judge them as*

worse. And that really was the beginning of the idea of scientific racism. And as science developed, and as [the science of] evolution in particular developed, humans, it was accepted with a great deal of pain, had evolved. It seemed obvious that there was a great ladder – and who was at the top? It was White middle-class men at the top and . . . Black African women in particular were at the bottom. Now that idea mixed race with class, and it came very much from the founder of my own laboratory, Francis Galton, who was Charles Darwin's cousin and was a perfectly good, respectable scientist who was interested in human diversity and human quality. His famous book was called Hereditary Genius, *and that's no mistake. He has a famous, or notorious, diagram . . . a map of the distribution of genetic abilities, as we'd say, with the ancient Greeks first, and then there's a big overlap with the English, and then we have the Asians, and after them the Africans, and then the Australians and then we have the dogs, et cetera. I think the development of scientific racism was actually not that closely tied to the abolition of slavery,* per se, *because the abolition of slavery was seen more as a moral imperative, and in some senses even as an economic imperative, than as a scientific one.*

Not until the 18th century, as Britain developed a 'home-grown' Black community, did change in the representation of Black people come about. William Hogarth's depictions of mid-century Covent Garden show for the first time Black characters who, although sometimes included for comic or ironic effect, are often present as individuals in their own right. Pictures such as 'Morning', 'Noon' and 'Night' offer us images of Black people simply as everyday citizens beside their White counterparts. Dignified portraits of Black individuals were not to appear until the 1770s and the rise to prominence of writers and society figures such as Olaudah Equiano, Julius Soubise, Francis Barber and Ignatius Sancho.

In the preceding two centuries representations of Black people in British painting tended to follow a predictable pattern, at least in portraits of the landed gentry. In the 17th-century portraits of Louise de Keroualle, Captain Thomas Lucy and the Duke of Schomburg the presence of a Black face served a singular purpose. Professor David Dabydeen explains:

> When you had your portrait done you had to have a status symbol present in the painting or, if you like, a shorthand indication of your wealth. By having a Black person there you were signifying not so much the source of your wealth, because you may not have wanted to broadcast that, but that you'd arrived in the society. You'd dress your Black up in an elaborate turban, polish his skin, clean his teeth, oil his skin, and impose upon him a certain sartorial elegance and have him standing by you, or else looking or kneeling at your feet, or else offering you a bowl of fruit. These are stock images. Or else serving tea whilst you're having a conversation with a fellow aristocrat – or a fellow social upstart, as it were. Eighteenth-century conversation pieces, as they were called, where you'd have group portraits of people conversing over coffee and tea, frequently had Black servants in attendance as

symbols of wealth, but also symbols of servitude. Sometimes you would get an interesting set of perspectives whereby the Black – the Black boy normally – kneels at your feet, looks up to you in veneration and even adoration, but you ignore the gaze by looking out of the painting towards the spectator. So in the very fact of ignoring the gaze, there's a kind of hierarchy of gazes. He is gazing at you and you're gazing at your spectator. So the Black figure is always being used as an indication of your privilege, your status and your superiority.

Before the Black person came into play, it was the dog that normally served this function. You'd get ladies with pet lap dogs with very rich collars, and that indicated a certain attitude to your animal – that you were wealthy enough to endow them with this kind of wealth. The dog didn't have the advantages that the Black person had. A dog couldn't really serve tea or coffee. Anybody could have a dog but in the eighteenth century you had to be rich to own a Black.

It is difficult to overstate the influence on British arts and culture of the influx of new wealth from the slave-owning colonies. The revenues from slavery are acknowledged as the greatest source of patronage for art in the 18th century. Alan Ramsey, the art critic and commentator on that period, wrote that 'the development of architecture, classical architecture in particular, all over Europe was a direct result of the revenues from slavery'.

For the planters and their families, art and the patronage of the arts were used not only to draw a screen of respectability over the sources of their wealth but to buy their way into the heart of that society which saw them as *nouveau-riche* upstarts. Just as their money had purchased political power in the Houses of Parliament, it would now enable them to assume the role of 'guardians of culture'. As Dabydeen says:

> *To patronise art you had to surround yourselves with painters, you had to get your portrait done, you had to encourage and patronise art and also music. You were showing that you were a person of taste rather than just a person of money. I find it rather interesting that in the eighteenth century the term 'patron' had a dual meaning. It could refer to an owner of slaves as well as a supporter of the arts. These people were the patrons of the eighteenth century in this double wing.*

He doubts if, without slavery, there would have been any development of Italianate tastes or the acquisition of thousands of old masters from Italy and France which form the collections of many museums and art galleries in Britain today.

> *People like Hogarth, Reynolds and Gainsborough benefited from the desire of the* nouveau riche *to portray themselves as landed gentry. So in a sense you could say that not only did the artists benefit from slave revenues but the nation as a whole benefited from the money because they were able to acquire art from abroad.*
>
> *I always think that there were two grand tours. There was the English gentleman who makes his grand tour to Italy and to France, to bring back home artefacts of that civilisation, which are mostly*

sculptures and paintings. And there was the other simultaneous grand tour, which is of Africans from the West Coast of Africa to the Caribbean and to the New World plantations. These two grand tours were intimately entwined. The first grand tour could not have existed without the second.

THE PEOPLE

Probably the least acknowledged aspect of Britain's involvement in the slave trade was the growth of a Black community in the British Isles – particularly in the slave ports of Bristol, Liverpool, London and, to a lesser and later extent, Cardiff – between the 16th and early 20th centuries.

THE FIRST BLACK BRITONS

Although Black slaves and soldiers came to this country during the Roman occupation – some authorities maintain that the Libyan-born emperor Septimus Severus, who spent the last three years of his life in London and York, was a Black African – plausible records of African populations settling here start with the arrival in the early 1600s of a number of Black men and women, some of whom were brought over initially as slaves but are listed in the censuses as musicians, servants, traders, students and sailors.

The first mention of the Black presence in royal records is of a certain John Blanke who was a 'Blacke trumpete' to both Henry VII and Henry VIII. It is almost certainly him featured on the embroidered roll in the Royal College of Arms seated on horseback among his fellow White musicians, playing a double-ringed French horn. His origins, whether a slave from West Africa or a free musician from the Iberian Peninsula, are unknown.

1555 saw the arrival of the first group of Africans in England. They were described as 'taule and stronge men who coulde well agree with owr meates and drynkes' but it was noted also that 'the coulde and moyste ayer dooth sumwhat offende them'. These men were brought over, not as slaves, from the town of Shama by John Lok, the son of a London merchant and alderman. They returned home after three months, their time in London having been spent learning English and easing into their future roles as intermediaries in the developing trade between England and West Africa.

Although the first official English slave expedition to Guinea took place in 1562, the fashion for titled families in England to have Black slaves among their household servants was not established untl the end of the century. From Queen Elizabeth's own household to that of Sir Walter Raleigh the Black page or maidservant became an exotic status symbol.

Documentation of 16th-century Black London is scanty but the community was subject to a set of responses that has conditioned the lives of non-White settlers to the present day. In 1596 Queen Elizabeth I sent an open letter to the Lord Mayor of London and to the mayors of other towns in which she stated:

> *Her Majestie understanding that there are of late divers Blackamoores brought into this realm, of which kinde there are already here to many . . . Her Majesty's pleasure therefore is that those kind of people should be*

sent forth of the land, and for that purpose there is direction given to this bearer Edwarde Banes to take of those Blackamoores that in this last voyage under Sir Thomas Baskervile were brought into this realm the number of ten, to be transported by him out of the realm. Wherein we require you to be aiding and assisting unto him as he shall have occasion thereof not to fail.

Worse was to follow. A week later a warrant was issued to all public officers requiring them to aid and assist in the arrest of

such Blackamoores as he shall find within this realm with the consent of their masters, who we doubt not, considering her Majesty's good pleasure to have those kind of people sent out of the land ... and that they shall do charitably and like Christians rather to be served by their own countrymen than with those kind of people, will yield those in their possession to him.

Even with the help of a Lübeck mercenary, Casper van Senden, this earliest attempt at repatriation failed miserably.

In 1601 the Virgin Queen issued a proclamation in which she reiterated her discontent that

great numbers of negars and Blackamoores are crept into this realm ... who are fostered and relieved here to the great annoyance of her own liege people, that want the relief which those people consume, as also for that the most of them are infidels, having no understanding of Christ or his Gospel.

Only in the 18th century did a Black community truly begin to take shape in Britain. Estimated at 15-20,000, it ranged from footmen and parlour-maids to princes and fencing masters.

London was a great magnet for escaped slaves. The principal centres of Black settlement in the capital were along the Ratcliffe Highway and in the 'Rookery' of Seven Dials, an area that was to stand until its demolition in 1852 to make way for New Oxford Street. The growing number of non-Whites coming into the Covent Garden area soon attracted the attention of the forces of law and order. Writing in 1768, Sir John Fielding complained about the negative social effects of Christianity and freedom on Black people:

> *There are already a great number of black men and women who have made themselves so troublesome and dangerous to the families who brought them over [to England] as to get themselves discharged; they enter into societies and make it their business to corrupt and dissatisfy the mind of every fresh black servant that comes to England, first by getting them christened or married, which they inform them makes them free (tho' it has been adjudged by our most notable lawyers that neither of these circumstances alter the master's property in a slave).*

These first Black communities in London produced a number of memorable individuals. The violinist George Polgreen Bridgetower was probably the most internationally famous Black person from that era. Born in 1779, he was the son of a Barbadian manservant to an Austrian prince and a native-born Austrian woman. As a child musical prodigy, he was brought by his father to play before King George III. He was taken under the wing of the Prince of Wales who appointed a series of tutors to further his musical education. He toured throughout Europe as a concert violinist and developed a friendship with Beethoven, whose Kreutzer sonata was dedicated to him in the words: 'Mulatto sonata composed for the mulatto Bridshauer [sic], the great mulatto idiot and composer.'

Almost as famous was Ignatius Sancho, the Black writer, musician, shopkeeper and man-about-town. Sancho, born on a slave ship in Cartagena, had come to London as a child. He entered into the service of the Duke of Montagu in his household in Blackheath. He taught himself by 'unwearied application' to read and write. He produced three plays for the stage, assorted poetry, three collections of music and a *Theory of Music*. In 1773 he married Anne, a Black woman from the Caribbean, and opened a grocery shop on Charles Street, now Charles II Street in Westminster. They had six children. He is best remembered for the publication of his *Letters*, which appeared in 1782, two years after his death. The collection was an immediate best-seller. His was a familiar face in London's artistic community. His portrait was painted by Gainsborough and the actor David Garrick was a close personal friend, as were the writer Laurence Sterne and the sculptor Joseph Nollekens. Writing on the excesses of the slave trade, Sancho said:

> . . . *you speak of the treachery and chicanery of the natives. My good friend, you should remember from whom they learnt those vices. The first Christian visitors found them a simple, harmless people, but the accursed avidity for wealth urged these first visitors (and all succeeding ones) to such acts of wanton*

cruelty that the poor ignorant natives soon learnt to turn the knavish and diabolical arts, which they soon imbibed, upon their teachers.

I am sorry to observe . . . your country's conduct in the East-West Indies, and even on the coast of Guinea. The grand object of English navigators – indeed of all Christian navigators – is money – money – money, for which I do not pretend to blame them. Commerce was meant by the goodness of the Deity to diffuse the various goods of the earth into every part . . . in Africa the poor wretched natives . . . are rendered so much the more miserable by what providence intended as a blessing: the Christian's abominable traffic for slaves, and the horrid cruelty and treachery of the petty kings – encouraged by their Christian customers who carry them strong liquors to enflame their national madness, and powder and firearms to furnish them with the hellish means of killing and kidnapping. But enough, it is a subject that sours my blood, and I am sure will not please the friendly bent of your social affections.

At the same time as these first expressions of Black thought entered general circulation, a small but vocal repatriation lobby began to make itself heard. One correspondent in the *London Chronicle* of 1764 expressed concern about the numbers of Black servants entering Britain:

As they fill the places of many of our own people, we are by this means depriving so many of them of the means of getting their bread, and thereby decreasing our native population in favour of a race, whose mixture with us is disgraceful, and whose uses cannot be so various and essential as those of white people . . .

They never can be considered as part of the people, and therefore their introduction into the community can only serve to elbow as many out of it who are genuine subjects, and in every point preferable . . .

Objections to intermarriage made by this unknown writer were seized upon by the pro-slavery lobby. One of its staunchest champions, the Nevis slave-owner James Tobin, aired the issue in a virulently racist speech in 1780 in which he raged:

The great numbers of negroes at present in England, the strange partiality shewn for them by the lower orders of women, and the rapid increase of a dark and contaminated breed are evils which have long been complained of and call every day more loudly for enquiry and redress.

An even harsher condemnation of mixed marriages was to surface in 1804 from a more unusual source. The otherwise radical writer and activist William Cobbett produced the following gem of invective:

Who, that has any sense of decency, can help being shocked at the familiar intercourse, which has gradually been gaining ground, and which has at last, got a complete footing between the Negroes and the women of England? No black swain need, in this loving country, hang himself in despair. No inquiry is made whether he be a Pagan or a Christian; if he be not a downright cripple, he will, if he be so disposed, always find a woman, not merely to yield to his filthy embraces, that, among the notoriously polluted and abandoned part of her sex, would be less shocking, but to accompany him to the altar, to become his wife, to breed English mulattoes, to stamp the mark of Cain upon her family and her country! Amongst white women, this disregard of decency, this defiance of the dictates of nature, this foul, this beastly propensity, is, I say it with sorrow and with shame, peculiar to the English.

The existence of Britain's long-standing Black community raises several questions. Who were these settlers? Where did they come from? And, most significantly, what has become of their descendants? One family's tale may serve to illuminate the thousands that are obscured.

THE BARBERS OF STAFFORDSHIRE

In 1752 a 15-year-old slave by the name of Francis Barber was brought to England by his master, a Jamaican planter called Richard Bathurst. Two years later, on Bathurst's death, young Francis was granted 'his freedom and twelve pounds in money'. After a spell at a Cheapside apothecary and a two-year period at sea on board HMS *Stag*, Barber entered the service of Samuel Johnson, the writer and lexicographer, as his valet and butler. Between 1767 and 1772 he was sent (at Johnson's expense) to Bishop's Stortford grammar school. In 1776 he married an Englishwoman, Betsy, who bore him four children – two boys and two girls. On Johnson's death in 1784, Barber was left an annuity of £70 and a gold watch.

The family settled in Lichfield in Staffordshire where, even so far from the temptations of the city, Barber's intemperate spending soon reduced them to poverty. One observer tells how they were 'improvident and strove to make a figure in the world, lived above their means and dissipated their property'. In 1793 an interview appeared in *Gentleman's Magazine*, which found him:

> *low of stature, marked with the small-pox, has lost his teeth; appears aged and infirm; clean and neat, but his cloaths the worse for wear; a green coat; his late master's cloaths all worn out. He spends his time in fishing, cultivating a few potatoes, and a little reading . . .*
>
> *Mr Barber appears modest and humble, but to have associated with company superior to his rank in life.*

In 1796 the family moved to Burntwood, a few miles from Lichfield, where Francis taught at the village school. He died in 1801.

Almost two hundred years and seven generations on, the Barber family still lives in Market Drayton, twenty miles from Burntwood. Dennis Barber is White but the memory of his Black ancestor is something he seeks to preserve, though it was not always the case:

> *It was not a subject spoken about outside the family. But we were made aware by our parents that our ancestor was Black and that we too could have dark-skinned children.*
>
> *The stories were really between my mother*

and father. My mother didn't like to hear any talk about Francis Barber. My father always raised it and always called him Mr Barber. My mother always used to turn round and say, 'Look, don't talk about that Black man in front of the children.' So of course, as we got older, the big worry from my mother was if any of my sisters, when they got married, were going to have a Black baby.

These fears, however, did not dampen Dennis Barber's enthusiasm and 20 years ago he began his own research into the life of his Black ancestor.

I had one or two people working with me in the same office and it was a secretary that turned round and said, 'I think we can find you something on your ancestry.' Her daughter knew of a book called Johnson Gleanings. She worked in the library in Stafford, and produced the book from the National Library up in Wetherby. I don't know if it's still there. But that started it off . . .

> *I wanted to find out more. Who was this boy born in a time of slavery and what did he actually do when he came to England? I think it would have been nice to find out where he had come from and who his parents were. But I wasn't able to get that far.*

Although Dennis Barber describes some members of his family as being 'quite tanned', he perceives himself as being 'quite White'. The last Barber of wholly African appearance was probably Isaac, Francis's grandson, who was living in Bursleigh in the 1860s. He was recorded as being dark-complexioned with a 'mulatto nose'. Of himself, Dennis Barber says,

> *I think I probably inherited quite a few things, especially the hair. It was only in the latter few years that I've noticed that my hair has gone quite frizzy. And it shook me a little bit, because one of my aunts was quite frizzy at a young age. And I wondered why. And then I thought back and thought, well, there must be something there, you know, with us coming from Mr Barber.*

The overall response from friends and neighbours to revelations of his ancestry was positive, but not his mother's.

> *To be quite honest about it, most people think it's wonderful. People that I worked with thought it was a fascinating story. But my mother was still living when I first started this and I used to get a lot of information from her because she was getting older, and we used to sit and talk about the various fathers and grandfathers and what were their likes and dislikes, how many children did my grandma have, and whatever happened to them. But if I turned round to her and said, 'Look, Ma, let's talk about the Black man,' she'd say: 'Don't you talk about that Black man to me.' And I think it's because she was the older generation – that there's that bit of fright, you know.*

Before long it became apparent that this story was not an isolated one.

I would say that now more than ever England has become very multi-racial. I would say there are many people that just don't know that there were probably coloured people in their family. I would say a lot of the English were Black in the very beginning. And now they really don't know and probably the only reason they don't know is because they've never been told and they've never researched. And when they have come to research they've come to a blank and couldn't find any further.

Ever since I've known about Francis Barber, I've always considered that, whatever little part it was, I'm still very English.

BLACK LIVERPUDLIANS

Many White British families are similarly researching and coming to terms with their African inheritance, nowhere more so than in Liverpool, a city which made its fortune from the slave trade and is home to one of Britain's oldest and least assimilated Black populations.

The first Black presence in Liverpool was in the early 1700s when the sons of several West African rulers were brought to the city to obtain a British education. The reasoning behind this was that the students would develop a favourable disposition towards British culture and, on attaining positions of authority, British trade. Portugal, Holland and France had been receiving African students for several decades. Britain and the American colonies were the last to take it up.

Liverpool's Black population was fairly low in the mid 1700s but was given a boost in the 1780s around the time of the American War of Independence. Black slaves had been encouraged by an edict of George III to defect to the British, and Black regiments were set up under British officers. When the colonial campaign collapsed the British forces withdrew, bringing large numbers, perhaps 4,000, of their Black ex-combatants back with them. Liverpool was the first port of call for several of the returning ships and many Black loyalists remained there.

The city's Black settlement has been a continuous presence for 200 years. During the 19th century a community developed composed largely of sailors and soldiers. Others came as servants and sometimes as slaves – the flotsam and jetsam of empire.

Ray Costello and his mother Edith, who describe themselves as 'a typical Liverpool family', are descended from one of the 19th-century pioneers. Outlining his lineage, Costello says:

> *My great-great-great-grandfather, Edward James, came from Scotland. He married an African woman during the time of slavery in Bermuda. Her son Francis James was the father of my great-grandfather, another Edward James, who came to settle in Liverpool around the time of the Crimean War.*

Edward James came to Liverpool as a 14-year-old. Slavery had been abolished in Bermuda in 1838, the year of his birth. In 1873 he married Harriet Gates from Barton in Cheshire. Ray Costello takes up the story:

> *She was from a Quaker family, which is interesting . . . If you look at the photograph, he was a six-foot-three person, an African-looking gentleman, and she was a*

*diminutive five-foot-tall ginger-haired lady. It seems
an odd match, but when you look at the Gates family
background, being Quaker and with this abolitionist
connotation and so on, you can understand why it
happened.*

Some of Costello's forebears by marriage were involved in
trading on the West African coast. His mother's great uncle,
Henry Brew, was descended from Richard Brew, a Manx trader
who, the family suspects, may have started out as a slave trader
before branching into what he describes as 'legitimate
commerce'. Richard eventually married into a noble West
African family and one of his in-laws, William Ansah, came to
Britain in 1736. As a high-born African William was feted by
London society. He won the nickname 'Cupid' due to his 'sweet
and amiable temper'. His portrait was published in the
Gentleman's Magazine and in 1750 a pamphlet was published
about him entitled *The Royal African: or, Memoirs of the Young
Prince of Annamaboe.*

Costello's Uncle Henry, however, arrived between the
First and Second World Wars and into hard times for Black
people in Liverpool where, despite his aristocratic African
connections and good education, he found great difficulty in
finding employment. He came to Liverpool as a student,
intending to move on to America, but he married and stayed.

Edith Costello is a living repository of family history. She grew up
in a poor White quarter, not in Toxteth which was the home of the
Black community in Liverpool. She was practically the only Black
child in her area and acknowledges that it was only as a teenager
that she became aware of a greater Black society:

Well, they were mostly White people, all my friends, at school and everywhere, and I was the only one coloured – you know, dark. And they used to ask me, how did you get dark? And I used to try and explain to them that my grandfather was coloured, you see. They used to accept me. They thought I was a mystery, so they liked me because I was a mystery.

I think it must have been on leaving school that there seemed to be a lot of coloured people. And some of them would look at me and would wonder if I had any colour, because I was a funny mixture. I was creamy olive skinned . . . People used to think I was Spanish. I had a lot of Spanish friends, but I was such a mixture.

It is this mix that now allows Ray Costello to identify his family as typical Liverpudlians.

Within a single family you can find West Indian, African, a White admixture, all sorts of things, all sorts of mixtures like that, and the reason is because Liverpool has such an old Black population and that sort of mixture is inevitable.

It's almost impossible to evaluate the exact number of interracial marriages in Liverpool. It's characterised by being a mixed population. But some of the Black genes, so to speak, have virtually died out. Or, if not died out, remained recessive within particular families. A classic case of this is a lady who rang me up, knowing that I'm a member of the genealogical society, asking me about Black ancestry

simply because she'd found a lady in Crosby whose
young daughter had sickle-cell anaemia. And nobody
knew where it had come from. But what had happened
was she'd been researching her own family history and
she'd missed a particular individual . . . .

It's very difficult to find what the Black
population of Liverpool is, simply because people have
become intermarried and there are some families only
now discovering that they do have a Black ancestor.

Despite the tradition of intermarriage, the Costellos maintain
that the city has still not fully assimilated its Black population:

There's an unmarked line down the middle of a road in
Liverpool. On one side is the all-Black area, and the
other side is the poor-White area. But Liverpool people,
Black Liverpudlians, have been born here since at least
the late 1700s, and there have been Black settlers
living here since at least the 1730s.

It's very much a contradiction that Liverpool
should have such an old Black population, an old
settlement. It's one of the oldest parts of Liverpool's
history – as a settlement. Many people came, for
instance, from Ireland in the 1840s as a result of the
famine, whereas the Liverpool Black population was
there a hundred years earlier.

I think the old Black settlement in Liverpool
still exists largely as a separate community. This town
still has problems regarding people moving into other
areas, it still has problems regarding employment and
people's perception. The Liverpool Black settlement

has not been assimilated in the same way as other communities who've come and settled in Liverpool from all over Europe.

These views are shared by Lawrence Westgarth, a descendant of another 19th-century Black settler, Robert Cox, who came to the city from Barbados in 1822:

In over 150 years of Black settlement in Liverpool the Black community has probably moved less than a mile from where it originally congregated. Black people's contribution to Liverpool's history has been negated to the point that a lot of people don't understand that Black people have been in Liverpool as a group for over 150 years. In Liverpool my family is up to its ninth generation, so when people talk about Windrush [the boat which brought Black emigrants from the Caribbean to England, in 1948] and the fact that we are now 50 years after Windrush . . . in Liverpool, it's not applicable whatsoever because this port has had a settled Black community for three times as long.

Where Westgarth's story differs is that, instead of claiming a regional English or British identity, his Black ancestry has encouraged him to establish links with the African Diaspora as a whole.

In many ways I suppose it's the same for everybody, in that a lot of people are very interested in where their origins are from — more so probably with people who are from the Black Diaspora because it's not so easy to trace, and the fact that most people who've come from a West Indian extraction don't really know their true cultural background. For people of African descent it's very important to try and trace back as far as possible to know where we actually came from.

I suppose in many ways it gives people a sense of belonging . . . that we do have a home. In order to get home, you have to know the way home. The way to do that, I feel, is by looking at my ancestors.

The fact that his ancestor Robert Cox found a home from home in Liverpool, a town which 30 or 40 years before his arrival was the centre of the British slave trade, is something Westgarth is slowly coming to terms with.

My feelings have changed over time. . . . It's probably understandable because as you . . . come to terms with such a terrible part of your own personal history, expressions and emotions are manifest in different ways. It's something that I've found hard to deal with. I've looked for solace by looking to people who I can identify with, who've been in the same scenario or have come from that same cultural background of being from the African Diaspora. But now I personally don't feel it's worth getting angry about. I feel that people need to channel their energy into ways which are constructive – by trying to find out about genealogies; by trying to look at that part of history when their ancestors were actually numbers, or became Coxes (as my family all became), either on a plantation or through marriage. And it's something that I channel my energy into with a great deal of enthusiasm.

This testimony, more than any other, may offer an important insight into the position of contemporary urban Black culture in Britain. Westgarth sees Liverpool not only as a strange phenomenon but perhaps also as an example of how Black British society may develop, given the decrease in immigration and increase in inter-racial marriage:

> *I don't feel that the lot is getting better for Black people. In Liverpool Black people have been here for so long but they've never been accepted. All you have to do is go into the city centre, you won't see many Black people even walking, shopping. You won't see any working in the shops. So even though Black people have been here for so long, in many ways they haven't progressed. And you can see that by the fact that the Black community hasn't moved from the area which it originally congregated in.*
>
> *Slavery has removed my ability to trace any connection with Africa. It's taken away my language, it's taken away culture, it's taken away every real aspect that I could ever use in order to associate myself with the mother continent of Africa. My father is from Jamaica, he has a name which is totally unrecognisable by any name that you'd find on the African continent. Why is that? Because he's named after a European who probably enslaved his family. Now in doing that, you know, he's totally taken away the connection. Because, over the centuries, everything has gone. The*

stories, the old traditions that were laid down, that were given – they're lost also.

Ray Costello adopts an intermediate position.

> *I would describe myself as Liverpool Black. Because we are a very mixed community. And we have a strong sense of identity, racial identity. But that is not to say that we would deny any of our other half-mixtures. That's very important. Because the Liverpool Black community has gone to both extremes during its life. There was a period when people would, if they were light skinned, deny their Black ancestry. And then during the '70s and '80s people went into 'Black and proud'. But there has been a period very recently when I think people are considering that they can't deny that they have, say, a White mother, a nice White mum, they can't deny that side of the family either. They must respect and acknowledge that they are a mixed community. But not forgetting the fact that the Black community has been treated very differently from the White community, and they are a part of that Black settlement.*

So, with one eye on the past, Black Britain's more recent settlers now look to the future.

THE PRESENT
DAY

Although 165 years have passed since Britain's official involvement in the slave trade ended, the questions remain: To what
extent do we still live in the shadows cast by those events? And
what becomes of us when we accept the slave legacy in its
entirety? The walk into light, either as a nation or as individuals,
will be neither short nor easy.

The overt traffic in human beings is over. But slavery,
though fading from active memory, lives on – signalling silently
from the bricks and mortar of Britain's great country houses and
from the squares of Bristol. It can be heard in the 'painful
ambiguities' of Caribbean art and culture. It is most visible in the
collapsing infrastructure of a depopulated Africa. Above all, in
Africa, Britain or the Caribbean, it is at the core of an identity
crisis.

Professor Gretchen Gerzina believes traces of 18th- and
19th-century interpretations of the African character are still
pervasive:

It's impossible to underestimate the power of those ideas. You may not think that a picture or a cartoon or a depiction in a novel that appeared 200 years ago could have any lasting impact but the fact is that they do. Caricatures and stereotypes had a specific political purpose at the time and, although that purpose may change, the ideas get passed on from generation to generation. So that when you see a film now that shows a Black woman in Britain who is highly sexualised and who is acting in inappropriate ways, you can hold up a picture from the eighteenth century that shows Black women depicted in exactly the same way and see that there has been a continuous threat of that that leads us up to modern times.

At the same time you can find very sympathetic depictions at that time which sentimentalise and infantilise; which make black people seem like they need to be taken care of or protected – and that comes right up into arguments about the welfare state. None of these ideas actually go away; they just alter and, I think, get perpetuated in ways that are very dangerous.

It's very hard to try to pinpoint when modern notions of racism began. They go hand-in-glove with the discovery of a wider world and then the political or economic uses to which it can be put. But what you do see is that the ideas of an earlier period that make people seem inferior get perpetuated in ways that change over the years but last. So that, if you have depictions of people as being enslavable, for example, then you may find that the same depictions appear

much later, centuries on, in similar ways. For
example, on television you often will see that a Black
person is a violent side-kick of a cop, and that this
person might act in ways that are a threat to society
even when they are the upholders of law and justice.
People begin to think those are true depictions but
those are not just modern ideas; they have a long, long
history.

> *Modern racism is very much rooted in the*
earliest encounters with a world that is not completely
White and which needs to be controlled in some way.

What the writer Fred d'Aguiar described as 'The Longest
Memory' appears also, in some ways, to be the faintest.
Amnesia, whether wilful or unwitting, seems omnipresent.
However, in Britain and throughout the African Diaspora,
changes are taking place. There is a new dialogue.

AFRICA

In West Africa many now look towards a second stage of
nationhood, this time embracing the complexities of the slave-
trading era. Kofi Awoonor, formerly the Ghanaian ambassador
to the United Nations, takes a pragmatic view:

> *I think the process of creating what is now Ghana*
must be traced back to that period. What we now call a
geographical entity, Ghana, is a conglomeration or a
collection of tribes and so on, who were at various
points in time part of this historical cauldron of
rivalries and wars and ethnic conflicts, which fed into
that large forced exodus of people.

Though people are coming to terms with the facts of pre-colonial slavery in some African societies, the overall effect of the Atlantic slave trade was devastating, particularly as it directly fuelled the ethnic conflicts which still bedevil the area. Kofi Awoonor continues:

> *Slavery existed in societies that had no prison systems. It was part of the punitive measures against criminal behaviour. And various kinds of things were punished by loss of liberty. So the slaves lost their liberty, they went away, maybe into the neighbouring state or the neighbouring nation – but only for a season. It was not a long-term loss of liberty. And the children of the slaves, of course, were never slaves in that context. With the transatlantic slave trade, you have a final separation. It was trade. And that drew into it almost every single original African nation. The small ones were brutalised. The big ones consolidated their power. And therefore some of the legacies of the nature of that particular trade are still with us, lingering with us in the difficult effort of building nations.*
>
> *It's not only Ghana. We have the same problem in Nigeria and in some of the Central African states in what is now the Congo, where ethnic rivalries came to the fore during the period of this trade – which fomented wars and brought in a cultural violence. And at a very intense level these issues or questions are being posed now.*

The loss to Africa is also being assessed in terms of its current crises of underdevelopment and underpopulation. In 1800 the population of sub-Saharan Africa and that of Europe were virtually the same. By 1901 Africa had about 100 million people fewer. With a shrinking population came a diminished skills base. Africans familiar with tropical medicine, mining, agriculture and metallurgy were highly sought-after by slavers trading with Spain's American colonies. Their absence would be felt for many generations to come. Meanwhile, much of African society had been destabilised. Kofi Awoonor:

> *For 300 years you had communities virtually on the run, moving from place to place. There's a great story of the African migrations of this period, which has yet to be told. And the evidence was still moving, as it were, from the Niger bend . . . the pressure from the Almoravids, from the coming in of Islam, and then the European transatlantic trade coming in from the coast. So people were looking for places of habitation. Then, of course, you have diseases and, with people being on the move, hunger and starvation. The entire refugee culture, as we see it in Africa today, began in that period.*

Traditional patterns of settlement, and with them indigenous methods of farming and political organisation, effectively ground to a halt during the time of the 'triangular trade'.

Only recently – and then with some trepidation – have the cultural implications of African involvement in slavery been examined in any depth. The main reason is guilt, the ever-present handmaiden of forgetfulness. It is described by Kofi Awoonor as a 'studied amnesia amongst the professional and middle classes'. Close on the heels of this condition comes the reluctance of African scholars to 'give ammunition' to some revisionist Western historians who see the identification of Black participation in the slave trade as a way of letting European society off the hook. Awoonor believes that honesty is the best policy. He emphasises the impact of the returnees,

> the African Americans who are coming home and asking questions. They're going into the slave forts and looking around and wondering. And of course they, more often than not, say, 'Well you sold us.' Yes indeed, they're very right. The African role in the transatlantic slave trade must not be swept under the carpet. This is what I keep on saying to my friends in the various cultural forums that we get engaged in. Let us accept that we were part of it. Because that is also part of the beginning of consciousness on our own part, that we did take part.
>
> We would be less than human if we hadn't taken part in that, because the greed factor was there. Kingdoms made money, they rose as a result of the trade. Powerful people, rich families . . . were created as a result of it – Africans who were active collaborators in the trade. And so, when we assess the story, I think sometimes this amnesia is engendered by a degree of guilt, which of course on the European side is a very powerful guilt today too, and I hope that in Britain they are also feeling the guilt. Because great wealth was also made for your great cities of Liverpool and Bristol and London.

But, though West African warlords grew rich from the slave

trade, it was Europe and not Africa that benefited from it in the long run. So how does this guilt register today in Britain's port cities?

BRITAIN

In the last few years there has been a shift in attitude towards the slave trade. Many Bristolians still appear loath to discuss certain aspects of the past and all too ready to let sleeping dogs lie. There is a reluctance to feel guilty for something that happened ages ago and a tremendous defensiveness as if to talk about the subject is tantamount to besmirching the name of Bristol and its inhabitants.

The historian and researcher Madge Dresser finds this disturbing:

> *It was never really publicly acknowledged in any ceremonies or plaques or what have you. There was a silence about slavery in some quarters and I think this was because there were still families who felt they had made their wealth from activities allied with the slave trade. And I think there was a political division. There were Tory interests that really didn't want to talk about it and Liberal interests which wanted to talk about the abolition and to condemn the slave trade.*
>
> *Since the 1950s there has been a new constituency coming into the city. Bristol has always been a city of immigrants, even in the eighteenth century, and new people – perhaps not feeling parochial loyalty to the city or perhaps feeling that it's best to confront the past – have confronted rituals like the Festival of the Sea, or even Cabot's commemoration, saying well,*

we're talking about the sea, we're talking about Bristol's role in the sea, why aren't we talking about the slave trade?

Overall, Europe transported some twelve million Africans, it's estimated, and of course many of the descendants of those Africans are living in Britain today, and I think it's important to understand how they got there and the dislocation and trauma that people felt.

In trying to comprehend contemporary British attitudes to its indigenous Black history, Professor Gretchen Gerzina finds parallels with previous eras:

People don't remember that Black people lived here. They don't want to know about it or they simply do not know about it. It's not comfortable to think that there might have been slavery at one time because it doesn't exist now and it doesn't affect you in any real way; it's not within you. I think the fear of the unknown lies in the idea that there might be more about yourself than you are willing to realise, because there was no sense that it was even possible. I think now we're really back to where we were several hundred years ago, before we had this importation of people. I see the same kind of phenomenon now – this denial of a history in England that has to do with race and with slavery. You get a real sense now that, if something happened before 1945, it didn't involve Black people in Britain; that when the Windrush arrived you had a complete infusion of Blackness which we now have to worry about. But in fact this is a fear that was going on for quite a long time, and probably we're in a very similar position now, in the last years of the twentieth century, to how England was in the mid-nineteenth century.

Some beneficiaries of the slave trade, like Julia Elton of the Elton dynasty, have never shied away from the source of their family's wealth. But, strolling through the gardens of Clevedon Court, she feels the weight of a second duty to history:

I think it's a miracle that we're still here. We don't own the house any more, it belongs to the National Trust, but we are still hanging on here by the skin of our teeth. I can't think of any other great eighteenth-century mercantile family that is still in the house that was bought with the proceeds of the seventeenth- and eighteenth-century mercantile trading.

My great-great-grandfather poured a huge amount of money into the public health of Clevedon. He built waterworks, he put in the main drainage, the sewage, the gasworks, he built the hospital, he was immensely concerned with the health of the town, and of course of his estate workers. He built the churches, the schools, I'm very proud of that. I think that they were a remarkable family, and we're still here, trying in a rather small way to keep it all going. I think continuity is a huge privilege nowadays. I think it's a privilege that we're still here. I don't know how long it will last. I hope it will see me out.

Slowly but surely, however, the feeling is taking root that the time has come to face the past squarely and fairly. Current strategies, such as the opening ceremony at the Pero Bridge, which spans St Augustine's Reach in Bristol docks, in April 1999, have moved away from the overt finger-wagging of previous decades towards a focus on the origins of the city's wealth – its beautiful architecture, its educational institutions and charities – as well as highlighting the hitherto ignored 300-year presence of its Black settlers. But anger still seethes beneath the surface, as seen in 1998 when the local group Massive Attack refused to play a concert in Bristol's Colston Hall because it was named after one of the city's great benefactors and slave traders.

THE CARIBBEAN

If Britons and Africans are struggling to graft slave-trade issues on to their 21st-century identities, they should look to the third point on the triangle: the Caribbean. There the social and economic impact of slavery has been examined most thoroughly. Moreover, the results of slavery on Caribbean society may be seen in terms of race relations, in terms of Black people struggling to rethink who they are, to build new identities and to find a place for themselves in a wider African world. Echoes of slavery can be felt in these societies every day – in the language, the literature, the music. Wherever there is creative expression, the presence of slavery emerges.

Caribbean society is still in the process of reinventing itself. There is a strong sense that emancipation was not the end of a process but the first step. Professor Hillary Beckles, Head of History at the University of the West Indies, explains:

All of the national heroes of [Barbados] are people who either fought against slavery or fought against the legacies of slavery. There are ten national heroes and all of them are persons who by virtue of their political interventions were fighting against White supremacy and struggling for democracy, for citizenship, for equality in this space we call Barbados.

On the other hand, we have a situation where the economic resources and institutions are still effectively in the hands of people of European ancestry. So we have a society where the politics is effectively managed by the African peoples and the economy is in the hands of people largely of European descent. So the process of creating genuine equality within all areas of life is not yet complete. We are not yet satisfied with the achievements. I think we still have a long way to go.

Diagnosing the British condition in the light of the Caribbean experience, Professor Beckles says:

I think British society now is struggling to come to terms with itself. It is coming out of that imperial history, coming out of that imperial circumstance, refashioning its own identity to see itself as a multiracial society, which indeed it is, and which is the result of that empire. So on both sides of the Atlantic there is a struggle to redefine identity. The British have to see themselves, I believe, in terms of that multi-culturalism; we have to see ourselves as still trying to uproot the privileges of White supremacy in this region.

After all, a multiracial society has some concrete advantages, as the geneticist Dr Steve Jones explains:

> *If you take humans as animals, British people as animals, any population as animals, the thing which is astonishing about the human race is how similar we are from place to place, not how different. Chimps, for example, from place to place are about fifty times more different than human beings are, and that's because we haven't been around for long.*
>
> *Britain was a rather homogenous society until quite recently. Most of our genes actually came from the Middle East with the farmers who came here 10,000 years ago. Naturally, it's now become much more mixed. From a genetic point of view, that mixing is going on apace. In terms of the intermarriage of people from different parts of the world, its frequency in Britain is higher than almost anywhere else. Now, I could make some rather liberal statements about what a wonderful thing that is, which in fact I believe, but what's interesting is what that's going to do to our genetic health, to the genetic future of Britain. It's probably going to improve it.*
>
> *Let's take a disease like sickle-cell. Now, if you've got only one copy of the gene, you're healthy; it doesn't have any effect at all. But, if you have two copies of the gene, then you're sick and it's a severe, damaging illness which is awful for the children who have it. The way you're guaranteed never to have two copies of a sickle-cell gene is if one of your parents is an African and one of your parents is a European. The*

same applies to cystic fibrosis, for which there is a gene common in Europeans. You can guarantee children without cystic fibrosis, if you're a European, by marrying an African. So all this intermixture is, I'm sure, going to improve our genetic health, not decrease it, and that's ironic when you think of all the horrors that were claimed to happen as a result of racial mixing. People were simply wrong.

Nevertheless, for many White British people the task of seeing themselves in multicultural terms may prove difficult. One such person, Janet Randall, who can trace her family back to slaves in Barbados, admitted:

I am sure that there are many White people who do not have any clue that they must have some coloured connection, because if you look way back, not just to the Caribbean islands but throughout the world, this has to be true. But where the slavery connection is concerned, I do feel that they probably wouldn't want to know. It's a hurtful subject and they would prefer not to know.

But for Robert Beckford the option of wilful ignorance no longer exists. In seeking out his slave-owning forebears, he has knowingly swum against the current of Black genealogical trends. His search has led him to a Pandora's Box of vital questions. Central to them all is the issue of redemption:

I was raised as an African Caribbean man in Britain and I've never had to think about White members of my family, it just hasn't really been part of my experience. But learning that I've got White relatives, possibly White relatives in Britain, I've got to redeem that history, find some way of embracing it rather than seeing it as something which is inherently wicked and terrible because it's the history of slavery. But I know that redemption isn't always easy. Often redemption involves some kind of restitution, something to make amends for wrong done.

What makes the Beckford story unique is that there are lots of Beckfords in Jamaica and White Beckfords in England. But they aren't a big enough family to get lost in the crowd. So there's a good possibility that the White Beckfords who are here are in some way related to the Black Beckfords in the Caribbean. So we're really talking about the history of a family that is both Black and White and living in Britain, but unaware of that fact. It's about missing relatives, and often people are walking down streets not realising that their histories interact. We're taught at school not to see Caribbean history or even British history as one which unites families, brings families together, and I suppose the Beckford story is about that. It's about Black families who are related to White people and vice versa.

Through his travels Robert Beckford has recognised the relationship – albeit muted, coded and mirrored – between what happened on the plantations during slavery and the treatment of Black people in the still racially divided culture of modern Britain. The task, as he sees it, is to redeem this history, so as to break the link or make it a more positive one:

> *I feel a sense of responsibility because this isn't just my story, it's the story of my ancestors, so I feel privileged that I have been given the opportunity to voice what happened to them. On the other hand, I feel it's not just my story because it's also the story of Black people with names like Dixon or Henry or Murray. I'm telling their stories as well as the Beckford story, because we all have this slave legacy, we all bear these names and many of us are trying to make sense of the names in light of the history.*